"Take a joyride with Lance and h[...]
thirty-cent gasoline and fifteen-cen[...]
endless possibilities for automotive adventures."
Bruce Caldwell, Editor Emeritus *Hot Rod Magazine*, author of *Corvette Milestones, Mustang Milestones, Hot Rod Annual, Bolt Together Street Rods*

"Lance Lambert is the Garrison Keillor of car stories. His nostalgic and chuckle worthy stories always put a smile on my face."
M.J. McDermott, KCPQ Television Reporter, author of *The Improv*

"Lance's book gives the reader a clear understanding of the love and passion that many people have for their cars, regardless if they own a multi-million dollar Classic, or a rust bucket sitting under a tarp waiting for restoration. Lance's stories provide laughter and a few tears as he shares his and his friends' automotive adventures."
Sandy Scott, Director of Operations, Petersen Automotive Museum

"I am a publisher, with more than 40 years of anticipating what readers will like. I can say from experience that they like the sometimes comical, always heartwarming stories that are penned by Lance Lambert. As a columnist for our chain of newspapers we always received positive comments from the readers. I understood, as I always looked forward to reading Lance's next column as well. This book is a culmination of some of the stories told over time about real places and people, who just happen to be car nuts as well."
Theresa Poalucci, Publisher, Journal Newspapers

"Compelling! Lance's book is a vivid and humorous look at 50 years of the memories of a true vintage vehicle legend. The vignettes are always evocative. A great read!
Kathleen Fullerton Bernhard, Ph.D., author of *The Invisible Woman*

"Lance has always had a love affair with old cars. There cannot be much doubt that unlike mortal man, he has well refined 30W oil running through his veins. As a prolific writer, emcee and TV host, Lance is everybody's 'in the know' and 'go to' car guy when they want the inside scoop. His stories are real and he has made it a point to document his adventures at every turn. His book is a 'must read'."
David Dickinson, Creator & Editor, *The Old Car Nut Book*

A few of the names have been changed in this book due to the activities described being illegal, embarrassing, incredibly foolish or, in many cases, all three.

Photo Credits: Frank Almquist, Christopher Andersson, Phyllis Bass, Brian Canfield, Karen Caropepe, Classic Cycle Bainbridge Island, Andrew Clinton, Dick's Drive-In, Bob Dillon, Bill Ducette, Etiquette Records, Evangeline Fabia, Frisko Freeze Drive-In, Joe Graziano, Connie Taylor Henderson, Paul Henderson, Annaliza Katakowski, Lance Lambert, Marconi Museum, Morti Morbid, North County Outlook, Dick Page, Phantom Coaches Hearse Club, Bill Pugnetti, Steve Puvogel, Seattle Metropolitan Police Museum, Darrol Smith, Tim Stansbury, Tacoma Police Department, Tacoma Public Library, Triple XXX Drive-In, Duane Vincent, Washington Dwarf Car Association, Robert Zenk and numerous strangers that responded to the request, "Hey, will you take a picture of us?"

Published in the United States of America

ISBN: 0-9844898-7-8S

ISBN-13: 978-0-9844898-7-9

Wooded Isle Press, 2400 NW 80th St., Seattle, WA 98117

Tim,

Just be glad I didn't write a story about you, me and that bus load of German hookers!

[signature]

FENDERS, FINS & FRIENDS:
Confessions of a Car Guy

Lance Lambert

This book is dedicated to Jan Lambert, my wife and best friend for the past 38 years. Her support of my various choices in life, both the good and the not so good, is incalculably appreciated. She has even forgiven me for having numerous affairs with Ramblers and Studebakers.

CONTENTS

Dedication i

Forward 1

PART ONE – BACK THEN

Treasures and Tar 7

Fill'er Up? 9

Syringe Solution 11

Gizmo Guy 13

Design Disaster 16

Bad Cadilluck 18

Grandpa's Garage 21

Model Behavior 23

Remembering the Rumble 26

Sirens and Haircuts 28

The Unknown Thingy 31

Wheels of Justice 33

Oh Chute! 35

Losers, Lambrettas and Ladies 37

My First Car Club 40

Pizza Sauce and 30-Weight Oil 43

Out of Odor 47

The Hole Story   49

Dave   51

Rocket in the Road   54

Beer Bowl 500   56

Twinkling Teeth and Taped Terror   59

Corvette Miracle   61

Rebecca's Run   63

Confessions of a Car Thief   65

Manly Mustang   67

Blissful Idiots   69

Fiberglass Fantasy   72

Dale Did It   74

Karma Triumph   77

Bad Mechanic; Worse Liar   79

El Camino Errand   81

Vans and Vanity   83

Persnickety Paula   88

That Was a Close One!   90

Idiot in the Arterial   92

Suffering From the Benz   94

PART TWO – NOT SO LONG AGO

Buried in the Barn   99

Insult But No Injury   102

Humpy   105

Bullion Bathed Benz   107

Bigger is Better   109

Father Dusters   111

A Final Rusting Place   113

Are You the Neighborhood Crackpot?   117

Audible Autos   119

Ballet Slippers and Magic Carpets   121

Cars or Conversation?   123

Dancing in the Neon   126

Invisible Rust   128

The Garage Monster   130

Hot Pursuit   132

Lowered Expectations   135

Big Wallets Required   137

Leaving the Lincoln   139

Savoring the Pits   141

Smarter Than Dirt   144

Car Friends   146

Confessions of a "Joiner"   148

A Gentleman's Ride   150

Perfect Parking   153

Roth's Wrath   155

Diamonds in the Dealership   157

Floating, Flying and Fraternizing   159

Garage Guys   162

Look But Don't Touch   165

Nerd Cars   167

What's That Noise?   170

Drive-In Delight   172

Road Rage Reflection   175

Right? Wrong!   178

213 Pounds of Love   183

T-Bird Tears   185

Ugly Eighties?   187

The "Y" Word   189

Grins in the Garage   191

Pedal Passion   193

Shag Carpeting and Fresh Eggs   196

To Build or Not to Build   198

Reunion Passion   200

Patina of Pooh?   202

Fortunate Five   205

Video Vehicles 208

Trophyitus 212

Vino or Vehicles? 214

Swap Meet Bargains? 216

Grubby to Guggenheim 218

Going Back 220

PART THREE – TV TIME

Whoops! I Dropped a Name 225

Landing Leno 230

Fire! Fire! 232

A Fan or Afraid 235

Your Last Ride 238

Second to None 240

Gears and Grins 243

Karma Cash 245

Vocal Viewers 248

Acknowledgements 251

About the Author 253

Also Available 255

Forward By
Don Weberg, Publisher, Garage Style Magazine

"Back in the olden days..." Growing up, this was a favorite expression of mine. It was a little perplexing to some adults who couldn't understand a boy of, say, 10 years old using the phrase, and then following it up with a statement that made sense. "Back in the olden days, it was so much cheaper to buy a candy bar, soda, and see a movie. It made life nicer because you could do more on the dollar."

I wasn't that insightful, but the fact that I liked old TV shows, movies, magazines, music, and, above all, cars, I was a little out of my element.

My friends were hitting the arcade, watching MTV, riding bikes, playing sports, and so on – I wanted to watch Fred Astaire or Sammy Davis Jr. tap dance; I couldn't wait to watch *The Three Stooges*, *The Munsters*, and *Gidget* on the weekends; the oldies radio stations were all my rage, and I really couldn't wait for my copy of *Hemmings* or *Cars & Parts* or any number of other car publications to arrive in the mail. Yes, I loved riding my bike, but outside of that, I was a little bit weird compared to my peers - video games were a little boring to me, computers were extremely boring to me, and sports couldn't be more idiotic. Why would I chase the ball when my dog could get to it and have it back to me before I could take my first few running steps? But, all of my interests had a simple nostalgic to them - a link to a time that I'd allegedly never participated in, yet somehow felt akin to. Nonsensical hocus pocus, right? Reincarnation? Perhaps. But regardless, I did, and still do, feel somehow akin to the olden days, and sometimes out of my element. As such, I strive to enjoy things at a slower pace, usually revolving around elements fixed back in time. Cars are huge to me for that reason.

In 1984 my Dad bought a relatively dilapidated 1965 Mustang coupe. In need of everything, it hid its deficiencies well, not revealing what a Pandora's Box restoration it would be until we began disassembling it and discovering first hand that project one couldn't be done without project two and three, and that all three couldn't be done without project A being done first. It went on and on, and a simple spruce up job turned into a three-year long restoration, with work being performed almost every day. The car probably should have been a parts car for another Mustang – but when it finally emerged from the garage in 1992, it turned out to be one of the sweetest little Mustangs ever to return from the brink. It's first year out it brought home a second place award against some stiff local competition, and emerged on the Ford scene with open arms. Gleaming with renewed chrome, deep Caspian Blue paint, a standard blue interior, standard hubcaps, whitewalls, a 289-2V, C4 automatic, and an astonishingly low 3.89 rear diff, the car surprised everyone by sporting all original components. During the restoration, and for some time before, I began scouring swap meets with my Dad, collecting various bits and pieces we knew the car would need – a set of original Ford horns, for example; the AM radio; and, of course, I fell in love with all the original advertising material. I was amazed at all the scenes Ford marketeers and Madison Avenue pros placed Mustang in – professional types, young adults, athletes, women, elderly people, and so on were all portrayed in various scenarios and it took me by storm. Here I was, in the late 1980's, pining to be one of those people back in the olden days. I wanted to be the smart looking guy in the suit and fedora arriving at a restaurant overlooking the Golden Gate Bridge with the gorgeous blonde; I wanted to be that guy in the helmet arriving at a checkpoint on some desolate mountain road; I wanted to be the surfer hitting the beach in the new-for-1965 Mustang. Somehow those ads, those scenes, those people, those cars each spoke to me, and I was again, hooked for all those things back in time. Back then, Mad Men understood and delivered on the mantra of, "Sell the sizzle, not the steak."

I grew up in a car house – Mom and Dad both raced cars, Dad built a fair number of hot rods and racing engines in his day, and an absolute ocean of their friends were somehow involved in the automotive hobby or industry. As such I was a victim of early car impressions. It's been said that my second word in life was 'Camaro,' but the first three cars I really remember pining over were the Pontiac Trans Am, Lamborghini Countach, and DeLorean. Later on, during the restoration of the Mustang actually, I became quietly enamored with the 1961-1969 Lincoln Continentals, those long, modernly-styled, slab-sided luxury liners that were the choice of America's elite. At least, according to the original advertising materials, they were. Interestingly, someone astutely pointed out that

I liked cars with weird doors. Fair enough – Countach, DeLorean, and '60s Continentals each boasted them. But it wasn't until the restoration of the Mustang that my car interest kicked into overdrive, and my interest of being in the 'back then' crystallized.

Lance and I met at a Packards International event in 2007. I was on the brink of publishing the first issue of Garage Style Magazine, and I briefly told him about the project. Interestingly he was not only open minded to the concept, but understood it maybe more quickly than even I did. I was producing a magazine about a space I always enjoyed time within – the garage – I was thinking about a magazine celebrating my favorite room, and betting that there were other like-minded people interested in a magazine that allowed us all to share our interest in our favorite room. But it was through some of Lance's writings that I began to understand why. I began to realize that I was among like-minded people in more ways than one. The nostalgic kinship that all of us car guys seem to carry in our souls, the thread, the connection – it became clear to me why the garage was such a favorite place for us. For me, Lance's writings reminded of the sizzle that we were, or maybe could have been or wanted to be; his writings take us back to presumably simpler times of dreamy days, giving us peep holes back to the olden days. For that reason, and so many others, I was humbled to write this forward, and hope it does justice to this latest Lance Production – maybe someday, someone will remember it and think about this great book from back in the day. Enjoy!

PART ONE

BACK THEN

Treasures and Tar

I grew up in a lower middle-class house in a lower middle-class neighborhood. I had no concept of middle or any class when I was young, so for me it was just where I lived. It was a middle-sized four-bedroom house built sometime in the 1920s. The home offered security, warmth and treasures--security because of my family, warmth because the furnace worked, and treasures because of what was in the garage.

The garage was not off limits to me; it was a place that I could linger in as long as I didn't mess up the various piles of my dad's junk. There were boxes of used mason jars, bags of rusty nails, piles of various lengths of angle iron, filthy canvas tarps, empty gallon glass bottles, bars of lead, cast iron kettles to melt the lead in, a huge block of hardened tar and many other castoffs and surplus items that my dad had scrounged.

He considered himself an expert handyman and utilized the loot in the garage for various projects. The rest of the family considered him an expert at incompletion. He was always starting a project at home that he never seemed to finish. The basement laundry room was never finished; the upstairs bathroom had a hole in the wall that was eventually going to be a laundry chute but remained a hole in the wall. The family room was never completed, the patio was never completed and the house remained half repainted throughout my childhood.

The garage's treasures brought me unending pleasures. The glass bottles, when filled with water, were great fun to use as targets for my slingshot. The lead bars always fascinated me with their incredible weight and the angle iron was used by my brother Jay to make the framework for a great backyard fort.

One of the best items in the garage was the block of tar. I'd use a length of angle iron to knock off small pieces and then chew them. Yes, chew the tar. It actually tasted good if the piece was very small.

Kids, don't try this at home, or in your garage either.

Another use of the garage was for the meetings of the "Back Ally Boys," a group consisting of myself and a few friends. We rode our bikes all through the neighborhood via the alleys. There was always something great happening in the gravel-covered alleys-- someone changing the oil in their car and pouring the old oil into the alley's dirt, a local teenager, aka my brother, siphoning gas from a neighbor's car, children jumping off a garage roof onto a pile of mattresses, and other activities worthy of being done only in an alley.

Then something really exciting began happening as I approached my teenage years; my brother acquired a 1939 Ford coupe, parked it in the garage and began altering it in an effort to make it a real hot rod. One necessary change was a new paint job.

One of the garage's treasures was a couple gallons of surplus army green paint. It took no time at all to turn the Ford's exterior into something that would make any veteran proud. No hot rods in town were painted U.S. Army green, and my brother's application of the surplus paint assured that this color choice would remain a rarity.

Danger was also an irresistible charm of the garage. The roof consisted of rotting timbers covered with sheets of disintegrating tar paper. Walking across the flat roof provided the opportunity to improve my balance as a result of trying to not step through the holes. Sitting on the edge of the roof was the perfect place to use my slingshot to shoot marbles into the walkway below.

The years passed and the garage continued its descent into disrepair. More holes opened in the roof, the garage door collapsed and, finally, we used the garage only for the storage of items waiting to be hauled to the dump.

A recent drive past the house revealed a bare concrete pad where the garage once stood. The memories of the garage still linger, especially when I smell hot tar.

Fill'er Up?

There are several things I miss about the 1950s. Near the top of the list is the neighborhood gas station.

On the corner of North 12th and Pine in Tacoma was a Signal service station that had not changed in decades. It had all the cool stuff you'd expect--new and used tires everywhere, rusty signs pitching tire repair and bulk oil, an ancient pop machine and, best of all, George. He was right out of Mayberry--dirty coveralls, pointed attendant's hat, grease under his fingernails and a great attitude. He believed that if you kept Mrs. Conklin's Buick running properly she'd keep coming back for gas and repairs. George felt that marking up items more than ten percent was criminal. And, much to my delight, he was willing to let a very young car nut kid hang out at the station.

I'd ride my Schwinn Black Phantom bicycle there several times a week just to watch him work. There wasn't a lot of conversation coming from George. Sitting quietly with him in the "office" shed waiting for customers to arrive was all I needed.

He finally put me to work sweeping the garage and parking lot. I was thrilled to be "working" at a real gas station and quickly worked my way up to official tire stacker, floor grease scraper and window cleaner. I was even allowed to visit the most mysterious place at any 1950s station-- the "grease pit." This was the pit in the concrete floor where you went to change a car's oil or work on the undercarriage. It was wet from spilled and leaking oil, a little dangerous and a place where only grownups were allowed.

I cared very little that George never paid me any money because being able to hang out at the station was payment enough.

In my eyes, the prestige job was actually pumping gas into

customer's cars. As far as I was concerned this was as good as being paid money. George and I would be sitting in the office when a car would drive up to the pump. I'd look at him apprehensively and wait for his quiet nod. When he nodded towards the car I'd race out and ask, "Fill'er up?"

Suddenly I was the most important 12-year-old kid in the neighborhood. Not only could I closely watch the gas pump gauge and stop at exactly $2.00, but I could remove the nozzle without spilling a drop. This was the most exciting car-related activity that I'd ever been a part of.

That summer was one of the best in my memory. As I grew older, I realized the need to get a real job if I was ever going to own a real car. I became a pin setter at the Elks Club bowling alley, got a paper route and did odd jobs around the neighborhood. Before long I had saved up $125 and bought a 1948 Chev Fleetline Aero Sedan.

I bet you can guess where I bought my first tank of gas.

Syringe Solution

I once drove a "fuel-injected" vehicle with a top speed of almost 10 miles per hour, and every two blocks it made me feel like both a race car driver coming into the pits and a school nurse during an anti-measles campaign. Let me explain.

My neighborhood in the 1950s and 1960s was filled with a large assortment of very small motorized vehicles. It seemed that every other house had a 12-year-old boy with a go-kart or "doodlebug" scooter. The go-karts usually were made of plywood and wagon wheels and powered by a surplus lawn mower engine. The "doodlebugs" were two-wheeled contraptions that, thanks to young imaginations, were as fast and exciting as any real motorcycle. We seemed to have no trouble driving these all over the neighborhood without anyone ever being stopped by the local officials.

My big brother and I shared a two-wheeled chariot that was blue, seated two and scooted, as a scooter should, along at blistering speeds of nearly two digits. However, there was one serious problem; it didn't have a gas tank. How, you ask, could it be operated without the second most necessary item of any powered vehicle?

My father, being a police officer, occasionally brought home surplus paraphernalia and confiscated contraband that was not usually found in my neighborhood's homes. These exotic items included a siren that a few years later found its way into the engine compartment of a friend's 1955 Ford, and a flare gun that, thanks to my poor marksmanship, started a nearby school's gymnasium on fire. Also found in my father's collection was a hypodermic syringe.

Now visualize this: I have a cool little scooter that has no gas tank and a dad who thinks I will probably live longer if he doesn't provide this missing item. What I do have is a syringe. So here's what I did. I filled a pop bottle with gas, inserted and filled the syringe and then squirted the gas into the fuel line of the scooter's motor. Then I pulled the rope start and off I went, scooting along with a bottle of gas between my legs, a dripping syringe in my hand and a smile on my face. Then, approximately two blocks later, I'd stop and do it all again.

Mr. Downey, one of the neighborhood dads, watched me go through this ritual and called me over to his garage. I didn't know if he wanted to help me fix the scooter's deficiency or if he just didn't think a 12-year-old kid with a syringe dripping gas was an asset to the neighborhood.

This dad, father of my friend Joe, was one of the neighborhood's cool dads and his garage was a place of wonder. It was very neat and perfectly organized, with enough space for two cars (huge by my neighborhood's standards), a hoist to remove engines from his endless parade of cars and, best of all, a pinup calendar that the neighborhood boys closely examined when he was not around.

We went into his garage, where he gathered up an empty paint thinner can, a couple of brass fittings and some solder. Within a few minutes his mechanic's magic transformed it all into a gas tank. Then he fastened the tank to the frame, poured in the remainder of the pop bottle petroleum and off I scooted on the scooter. Mr. Downey, no doubt, felt that he'd saved me from some petroleum-based disaster. I felt honored that Joe's cool dad had allowed me to enter his garage of wonder, and yes, I did glance several times at that wonderful pinup calendar.

Sadly, currently there are no kids currently puttering around my neighborhood on homemade scooters. There are, however, several cool dads with cool cars and cool garages. Fortunately, there is no goofy 12-year-old syringe-wielding kid living in the neighborhood.

Gizmo Guy

My abilities as a mechanic are, at best, non-existent. I give my brother Jay full credit for my early years of auto mechanic non-training.

Jay's 1939 Ford Standard Coupe was always in need of fixing. It was so in need of fixing that it was barely a 1939 Ford and more a collection of auto and hardware store gizmos covered with a coat of surplus army green paint.

Gas pedal and throttle linkage? Not needed! My big brother just got me to hang out of the hole where the windshield used to be and work the throttle linkage gizmo by hand. It was an ingenious system; he'd yell "more," and I would jiggle the gizmo and make more gas go into the carburetor. He'd shout "stop," and I'd stop jiggling. Granted, we were not driving down an interstate or a main arterial in this manner, just around the block, but the puzzled neighbors thought my brother and I were perhaps not the brightest of the Lambert siblings.

Jay's ability to make nearly nothing out of nothing was admirable. It seemed he only drove the '39 Ford to find out if it would function properly after his latest swap of an auto part for a piece of lawn and garden equipment or a vacuum cleaner part. On one such drive, my big brother handed me the steering wheel. I don't mean that he allowed me to drive; I mean that while we were driving down the street he removed the steering wheel from the steering column and handed it to me. He decided that the best way to attach a 1956 Oldsmobile steering wheel to a 1939 Ford steering column was with a very large bent nail. I advised him, as best that a little brother is allowed, that it might be wise to replace the steering wheel before we made an uninvited visit into a neighbor's living room. What he lacked in mechanical ability he made up for in manual dexterity. He had the steering wheel back on and the brakes applied before we were in any real danger.

Please don't misunderstand our brotherly relationship. Jay loved this little brother very much, even though his green monstermobile was a threat to my life.

He and his friend Dave Wonders were working on the car one sunny Saturday afternoon and I asked if I could help. Jay told me to attach the exhaust pipes to the frame using the finest equipment available from his vast supply of tools and "auto parts." In one of my hands he placed a set of worn pliers and in the other the finest quality wire coat hanger. Yes, the same type of hanger that usually resides on your closet floor.

Under the '39 I crawled, fully equipped to tackle this highly technical assignment. I bent, wrapped, pulled, adjusted and managed to attach one exhaust pipe, not realizing that in a few seconds my brief lifetime was possibly reaching its finale. While attaching the other exhaust pipe I was suddenly looking death in the face. Actually it was the bottom of my brother's shoes that I could see through a portion of the rusty floorboards. It seems he forgot about that his darling little brother was busily working under his feet. He started the engine and put the coupe into gear. Here comes the good part! His friend Dave, being of the Wonders' family lineage and, as a result, having a higher IQ than the combined Lamberts' IQ, grabbed my ankles that were attached to my legs that were hanging halfway out from under the car. He gave a very hard pull and succeeded in extracting me before Jay succeeded in turning his little brother into a two-dimensional simulation of his little brother.

Thanks, Dave! Last I heard of life-saver Dave, he had moved to Southern California and was saving souls rather than lives.

My brother realized that perhaps repairing automobiles was not his strength. Suddenly the '39 Ford was gone and Jay was rebuilding a 650 Triumph Bonneville motorcycle in the basement. He was definitely better with motorcycles and, as a bonus, pyrotechnics. I won't bore you with  the story of how our house was set on fire as a result of my brother trying to ride the Triumph up the basement stairs.

Design Disaster

My father wanted me to love her, my mother didn't approve of her, and I didn't want anything to do with her. Before I tell you about "her," let me explain that I had a total obsession with automobiles as a 14-yearold boy. Many an issue of *Hot Rod* and *Rod & Custom* magazines disintegrated under my repeated page turning and the top of my desk was covered with partially built model cars. I spent a few Saturday afternoons standing on busy street corners with my friend Dale while we, as best we could, identified every car that drove past. Local car dealers knew to lock their doors when this pesky kid bicycled onto the lot and begged for any new car literature.

Yes, my love and fascination for automobiles was firmly ingrained, but my father was asking too much of me. "Her" was the homeliest car ever designed and actually manufactured. It's a good thing that the 1949 car-buying public was purchasing anything available, because that 1949 Dodge Business Coupe had a most unfortunate design.

From the front it looked like Jimmy Durante on wheels: a huge nose and too much forehead. From the rear, and the entire car was mostly rear, it seemed that you were gazing at the Goodyear blimp. That car could house a small family and still have enough room remaining for all the relatives to attend Thanksgiving dinner. This was one mud puddle ugly car.

Dad brought the car home, parked it on the front parking strip, pulled off all four wheels and left it sitting on blocks. Do you remember those inconsiderate neighbors who lived down the street? They were us. He put the wheels on some other, needier vehicle and left that dreadful Dodge to rot on the roadside. Then a brilliant idea occurred to him: he had a kid who was crazy about cars, a problem sitting in front of the house and a wife who was bugging him to "Take out the garbage, and that includes that horrible car." The light bulb went on and, at the ripe young age of 14, I became the dreadful

Dodge's new caretaker. My meager possessions now included a business coupe that had no wheels and was not fit for any self-respecting chicken to use as a chicken coupe. Thanks, Dad.

What was I going to do with this eyesore? I must have been a very good boy because the car gods decided to smile down upon me. The first day of ownership dawned with this unfortunate new owner sitting on the front porch staring at the neighborhood embarrassment and trying to figure out what to do with it. Having any car at that age was something that should have been appreciated, but this car could not be appreciated. Just then, two older teenagers walking down the street spotted the car and asked me if I knew who owned it. They were a bit surprised when someone younger than they replied, "It's mine."

Then they asked the sweetest question ever spoken: "Is it for sale?"

Going to church had finally paid off! Trying not to wet my pants with excitement, I shrewdly responded, "Yes, yes, yes it is definitely for sale. Do you want it? I'll make you a really good deal. Please, don't be afraid to make any offer. I'll consider any reasonable offer!"

This shrewd method of selling cars has stayed with me right up to today and always assures that I take a huge loss on any car that I sell. But here was a chance to sell an unwanted car that I had not invested a single penny into. They offered $50 for it! This was 1961 and $50 could buy a car that was much more attractive than a de-wheeled 1949 Dodge Business Coupe.

Dad said it was OK to sell it, but the look on his face gave away his true feelings. He realized that his ungrateful kid was giving away the gift of a first car, any hopes of father and son working on it were dashed and, most of all, the Homer Simpson in him was screaming "Why you little.........I want that fifty bucks!" Dad stayed stoic about it and said that yes, it was OK to sell the car, so it was sold to these two obviously visually impaired teenagers.

The cash was deposited into my slowly growing car savings account and a couple of years later was used to buy a truly attractive 1948 Chevrolet Fleetline that self-destructed one week after its purchase. At least it was still wearing its wheels at the time of its demise.

Bad Cadilluck

It wasn't that my sister was such a bad driver; it was that she and the Caddy had such bad luck.

It was a very exciting spring day in 1957 when my dad brought home our almost-new car. There, parked in front of our modest home was a beautiful 1956 Cadillac Coupe DeVille. How could my father have afforded a nearly new Cadillac on his police officer's wages? The 1950s status symbol belonged on the other end of town, not in our lower middle-class neighborhood.

A close examination of the yellow and white Caddy revealed the answer.

According to Officer Lambert, the previous owner had left her two children inside the car while she went shopping. These two temporarily orphaned siblings needed to find some way to pass the time, so they began examining the Cadillac's accessories. Perhaps they began pushing, pulling and twisting everything on the dashboard until one of the chrome-plated knobs popped back out. Curiosity likely made the children look closer at the knob, and when they removed it, they learned that it was hot enough on the end to burn their fingers. Yes, their dashboard dallying resulted in their discovering the cigarette lighter. Their activity then changed from a journey of discovery to a display of artistic creativity. The two children began making small cigarette-lighter-sized burns throughout the interior. Small circles now adorned the dashboard, door panels, seats, headliner and most every other horizontal or vertical surface.

That is how Dad's police wages could pay for a nearly new Cadillac.

The indignities suffered by the Cadillac did not stop with the change of ownership. Soon after its arrival, my sister Judy passed her driving test and received her driver's license. What for some is the beginning of one of life's greatest pleasures, driving, was the beginning of the Coupe DeVille's demise.

It seems that my sister could not be within visual sighting of the Cadillac without something terrible happening to it.

Its first taste of indignity was when my dear sister, while traveling down the road minding her own business, was suddenly looking at the Cadillac's hood. No, not looking down at the hood, but looking straight ahead at the hood. It had flown open and was now attempting to drape itself across the windshield like red satin sheets across Marilyn Monroe. No, it was not sis's fault; it was just bad luck.

Our father, for whatever reason, chose not to have the hood repaired. That was a bit of a mystery because he also sold insurance part time, and it was reasonable to assume that the Cadillac was insured. Insurance or no insurance, the poor DeVille now held its head, and hood, up with a little less dignity. It was now marred both inside and out. But the great old Caddy kept on ticking, unaware of the additional tragedies that it still had to endure.

Not long after the hood's vertical travel, the Caddy received its next injury.

My big sister was driving through the neighborhood and minding her own business when she came upon a car minding its own business, parked in a very unfortunate spot. There were about 79 inches of space to pass the parked car, but a 1956 Cadillac is 80 inches wide. Our Caddy and the parked car met, exchanged a loud greeting and decided to embrace. The Coupe's first injury was to the front, and now it had an additional injury on the side. Don't worry; the rear end's time was coming. And, of course, dear old Dad again did not have the car fixed.

Big sister Judy borrowed the battered Caddy to attend a dance at our church. She arrived at the church and began participating in the evening's closely monitored dance. The latest dance crazes were attempted along with forced participation in a dance requiring the participants to put both their left and right feet in and "shake them all about." All was well until a crash was heard above the sound of the music.

Apparently a well lubricated nearby resident mistook the rear of our poor Cadillac for the entry to his garage. The amount of damage was incredible, resulting in the rear end of our abused auto looking like an accordion.

There were two amazing results to the Cad's latest bad luck. Amazing result one: the drunk driver was unhurt. No doubt he was happy to be alive, but unhappy about being handcuffed and helped into a black and white Ford police cruiser. Amazing result two: the Cadillac was still operable.

You guessed it; Dad again did not have the damage repaired. From that point on the Lamberts, with the exception of the elder Lambert, refused to be seen in the car.

Did the insults to the Coupe DeVille end? Was it to be parked in the back yard and allowed to slowly be reclaimed by nature? No, there was still one final insult (coupe de grace?) to the honor of the Cadillac.

Dad was "encouraged" by the family to sell the battered hulk, and he actually found someone interested in owning what was left of the car. I swear on a pile of 1950s *Rod& Custom, Hot Rod* and *Car Craft* magazines that the next part of this tale is true. The poor Cadillac, beat up from the day it left Detroit, was traded for a bowling ball and a box of chocolates. Straight across: coupe for caramel, fins for filberts, transmission for truffles and a three-way power seat for a three-holed sphere.

Please, wipe away your tears as I have mine. That Caddy lives on in my memory as the branded beauty that I first saw parked in front of our house.

Grandpa's Garage

Jack Mann, my grandfather, fulfilled the duty held by everyone's grandpa; he had a garage that was full of wondrous items. The workbench top looked like the floor of a 100 year old country store; a shiny surface of hills and valleys created by numerous decades of projects and repairs. The surrounding storage shelves and drawers were well worn and well organized. There were jars everywhere filled with nuts, bolts, screws and everything else that might be needed for a future project. Thanks to his inspiration I have a good/bad habit of dismantling various machines, be it a burned out blender or a dead computer. I save every nut, screw and odd shaped piece of plastic or metal that might be of use someday. Grandpa didn't seem to throw anything away and, as a result, eventually he provided me with a great museum of historic hardware.

Entering his garage was a bit like entering the house of Bilbo Baggins, the main character in the Hobbit adventures. The garage was a bit dark with lots of things brown in color; exposed wood beams overhead, light streaming through dusty windowpanes, and mysterious and magical things in jars. Next to a jar of brass screws was a jar of rusty screws. Though rusty, grandpa knew that the screws would be acceptable for various projects. Bent nails were saved to later be straightened in a huge vice. Small amounts of leftover paint were combined, resulting in canisters of light green, grey or brown paint.

The metal shelving saved from an old refrigerator eventually became the grill of a homemade barbeque. The intricate cardboard boxes, previously used to deliver beer to the tavern he owned, were now painted different colors and filled with things too valuable to throw away but possibly never to be used.

One special item on a shelf was a thick scrapbook filled with illustrated articles cut out from issues of *Popular Mechanics* that were published as far back as 1923. The scrapbook's cover is adorned with "Jack Mann 1923" and the frayed edges attest to it being frequently referenced.

Grandpa Jack's garage was not rundown or dirty but, instead, was more like a well loved and well used old car. It was useful and continued to display dignity and good character. It would provide you with what you needed as long as you provided it with the proper care.

Grandpa, like all grandpas, eventually passed on. Grandma moved into a retirement home and the house and garage were sold. The structures were eventually torn down and replaced with a medical facility.

Many of the treasures in grandpa's garage now reside in my garage. All projects needing a hammer are completed with his hammer featuring a handle carved on one side with "Jack Mann" and "2-26-46" on the other side. Some items stored on my shelving are protected in a Regal Amber Brewing Company box partially painted a light brown. A metal and glass oil dispenser, once filled with cut up lengths of coat hangers, now sits proudly on display.

The most appreciated item retrieved from the garage is the "Jack Man 1923" scrapbook. In it you'll learn how to transform your car into a simulated locomotive that "Speeds Tourists Across the Nation," or how to route you car's exhaust system tubing through the interior so it acts as a heater when "…the exhaust gases circulate around the car."

Non-automotive projects include musical instruments made from dried corncobs, how to turn tobacco cans into door hinges, and a fish scale remover made from a rat trap.

The time spent in my grandpa's garage is now seen through the soft focus provided by the passing of time. But no matter how romanticized the memories are, I know that Grandpa is proud that his grandson is carrying on his salvage and save campaign.

When my time comes to pass through the "Pearly Gates" I'll check to see if the hinges are made from tobacco tins and if the angel's harps are made from corncobs. If so then I'll know that grandpa is waiting there for me.

Model Behavior

The love of old cars hits many people at a very young age and continues to increase as they get older. A lot of the participants in the old car hobby got their start by spilling paint, ruining shirts and inhaling toxic fumes. No, it was not some illegal activity. It was building model cars.

As a boy growing up, I, like most of my friends, found various ways to make some spending money. First it was scouring the neighborhood in search of pop bottles to cash in for two cents each at the local Thriftway. The climb up the economic ladder continued as I cut grass and did odd jobs in the neighborhood and waited until I was old enough for the opportunity to "make some real money."

Every kid in my neighborhood sought the same financial goal--to get a newspaper delivery route. This money-making method always seemed available to anyone who tried hard enough to be a "paper boy." I acquired a route in the neighborhood that included 80 homes in an area of three blocks by four blocks. That doesn't sound like a large area, but it took about an hour every day to get the papers, load them in the double bag (one bag in front, one bag in back), fold the papers and toss them onto porches rather than into the bushes. It was a seven-days-a week job, and anyone with a paper route was grateful to have this source of income.

At the end of every month the subscribers paid their bills and I was left with about $30 to do with as I pleased. One of the pleasing things I did every month was buy one or two model cars. I usually purchased an AMT "3 in 1" kit for $1.25.  They were excellent quality kits and AMT offered a huge selection of cars. If money was tight, I'd settle for a cheaper model of lesser quality that was usually poorly made and required a lot of work to correct the manufacturer's mistakes. My AMT 1962 Pontiac Gran

Prix convertible won a first place award (the award was another model) at the local hobby shop, and a few months later my six-cylinder-powered dragster also brought home a first place award of another model. Thankfully the awards were AMT kits and not piles of poorly produced plastic pieces found in the cheaper kits.

What was it about building model cars that was so fulfilling? Everything! I loved the solitude of sitting in my room and building a kit while listening to the voices of Elvis and Chuck Berry spill out of my radio, also purchased with paper route earnings. To this day I can remember the specific model car I was working on when an oldies station plays a "Top 40" hit from the late '50s or early '60s.

My best friend Dale also built model cars and we each felt that we were a much better model builder than the other. Occasionally we'd sit in one or the other's bedroom and work on our models together. "Look how good my paint job looks," I'd say to Dale. That was usually followed by a remark from him such as, "Why is there glue smeared all over it? Look how the paint on my model shines."

Dale and I are still good friends and I'm still convinced I was a better model builder than he.

Many good things come to an end, and eventually building model cars stopped being my favorite pastime. The enjoyment was subdued by turning 16, getting a driver's license and replacing the little table-top cars with full-sized cars. Money saved from my paper route and odd jobs resulted in a bright yellow 1948 Chevrolet being parked in the driveway.

Decades have passed since then and I have purchased and

sold dozens of old cars. My love of model car building has never left and, thankfully, has emerged from hibernation and is again providing me with hours of pleasure.

There is a small room off of

the Lambert garage that Mrs. Lambert and I call the "Car Den" and a friend refers to as, perhaps more accurately, "Lance's I Love Lance Room." It is filled with hundreds of automotive books and decorated with old photos, automotive memorabilia, awards from car shows and several small-scale diecast cars that cost more to purchase than what I paid for a few full size cars.

Once again I can be found gluing plastic fenders together while listening to "Cathy's Clown" by the Everly Brothers or mounting the tiny tires on tiny rims while listening to Ray Charles belt out "Hit The Road, Jack." Sitting on a shelf in the den is a recently completed AMT model of a 1949 Mercury, and on the desk is a partially completed 1940 Willys.

My feeling of pleasure now is no less than what I felt 50 years ago.

Watch out, Dale! I'm back.

Remembering the Rumble

It was a quite Saturday afternoon and I was doing what any normal 12 year old kid would be doing; watching cartoons.

Suddenly the world outside sounded like it was exploding. The windows began to shake and my heart began to race. This was no lawn mower engine starting or a neighbor using a chainsaw; it sounded more like a B-29 Superfortress getting ready for takeoff. It was the most beautiful sound in the world.

I jumped up from the couch and ran to the door to see what was causing a minor earthquake on my street. There before me rumbling down the road was a real dragster! It was a real dragster like the ones in the car magazines that were traded amongst my car crazy buddies. This dragster was long, lean, sounded mean and had "Snoopy 2" painted on the sides. The exposed Oldsmobile engine had 8 exhaust pipes pointing at the sky and belching out fire and smoke. The long metal tube frame with "slicks" on the back and skinny tires on the front, along with the very high horsepower "mill", meant that there was only one purpose for this vehicle: traveling one quarter mile in the shortest possible time. This was in 1960 when a good dragster traversed 1,320 feet at 125 miles per hour and a great dragster at 175 miles per hour. Don Garlits, perhaps the most famous drag racer in history, set the world's record in 1960 at a speed of 195 miles per hour.

Previously the most exciting thing that had ever driven down our street was a neighbor kid's go-kart that was powered by a McCulloch chainsaw motor. My friends and I envied that lucky kid for having the coolest go-kart and coolest dad in the neighborhood. He dropped down one rung on the coolness ladder when this real fire breathing "rail job" came slowly rumbling through the neighborhood.

This sight was unusual and unbelievable but there it was before my eyes. Seeing "Snoopy 2" sauntering down our street was an amazing sight.

A little investigation revealed that it was in the neighborhood being worked on by the chainsaw powered go-kart pilot's dad. This put that kid right back up to his former spot on the coolness ladder.

No doubt the "Snoopy 2" is long gone but it will never be forgotten by this car crazy kid.

Sirens and Haircuts

Growing up with a police officer for a dad was great. There were definite advantages, including the numerous times his co-workers overlooked some of my less-than-civic-minded activities ("You're Rex Lambert's kid, aren't you? Go straight home, young man, and don't let me catch you doing this again!").

Another fun thing about being a cop's kid was the stuff in our basement. It was cop's booty and was a constant source of entertainment, surprises and, occasionally, a major score. Define score? How about a huge chrome-plated, bullet-shaped siren from the fender of a police car? I gazed at it and wondered what heroic and great adventures it had been on, how many bad guys it had chased and how many times it summoned excitement and respect from all who heard it. I wanted this siren. I also wanted the excitement and respect it commanded. I was not to be denied.

At the age of 14 I worshipped a neighbor kid named Ricky. Every kid in the neighborhood looked up to him. He was a tall, blond and handsome 15-year-old kid who wore a leather jacket. That was a hard combination to top. He also had a beautiful 17-year-old sister who was tall and blond. Everyone commented on how much she resembled Marilyn Monroe.

The pecking order in the neighborhood revolved around who Ricky decided was his best friend at any particular time. For a while it was me. One of the benefits of being Ricky's favorite was that you got to hang out with the older guys. Jackie was so cool that he was accepted by the guys old enough to own and drive cars. I'm talking about real cars--spinner hubcaps, side pipes, rolled and pleated interiors, lowered, nosed and decked cars. The real thing--CARS! These guys liked Ricky because he was cool, and because getting on the good side of him provided the opportunity to get on the good side of the neighborhood's Miss Monroe.

So there I was, hanging out with Ricky and these older guys with cars. It was a Saturday afternoon and we were lounging in Ricky's garage when Dick pulled up in his 1955 Ford. It was a white two-door sedan with spinner hubcaps and side pipes. I wanted to impress everyone so I asked, "Why don't we install a siren in your car?" They were impressed that I had access to a siren and agreed that my suggestion was a good one.

Dick's Ford resembled an unmarked police car of the type that the Tacoma Police Department was still using at that time. This was 1960, but the police department's fleet included a few 1955 Fords. Dick's car was the right color for a police car, it was the right make and model for a police car, and with the siren it would be even more like a real police car.

This kind of activity nowadays will, justifiably, get anyone as foolish as we were in a huge amount of trouble. But back then we considered it, though still very illegal, was just a notch or two above our average teenage mischief.

We drove to my house and I pilfered the siren from Officer Lambert's "home office." A drill, a few sheet metal screws, some wire and several willing hands resulted in an installation to be proud of. Push the Ford's steering wheel horn ring and from inside the engine compartment the siren wailed.

By now it was late afternoon and the fun was about to begin. I raced home, gobbled down my dinner and told my mother that I was going to a double bill at the nearby Sunset Theater. I headed back to Ricky's house, where Dick, Ricky, another guy and I climbed into the Ford and set off for the evening's entertainment. We began pulling over cars. We'd pull up behind someone, hit the siren and laugh when they pulled over to the curb. We'd drive by them and wave. Then we'd pull up behind another car, push the horn ring and that car would pull over.

We then drove to a couple of Ricky's girlfriend's homes, hit the siren, waved and quickly drove away. This was not Boy Scouts, 4H Club, a church dance, hoops with jocks or sitting in the library with the honor roll students. This was a lowered, white 1955 Ford Mainline two-door sedan with spinners, side pipes AND A SIREN! This was real fun--real illegal but real fun.

We managed to keep this up for a couple of hours. Finally the fun was diminishing and it was time for me to return home from my alleged evening at the movies. I said goodnight to the guys and then went into the house and told my mother that I was really tired and was going straight to bed. If I went straight to bed my mother would not be able to tell that I had spent the evening inside a cigarette-smoke-filled car pulling over innocent civilians. Something about the quick move to my bedroom, sincerity in my voice, and being my mother's favorite made it impossible, or so I thought, for her to know that I'd been smoking and engaging in some truly illegal activity.

I climbed into bed and was contemplating the evening's adventure when I heard a siren somewhere off in the late night darkness. It was THE siren. I had been listening to it all evening and  was tuned into its exact tone. However, after hearing THE siren I heard another siren. Not THE siren, but a different siren. Yes, they were busted.

In 1960 Tacoma, anyone arrested who was less than 18 years of age was given a free haircut. Actually, about three haircuts were administered, all at the same time on the same head. This type of haircut is currently popular with a small segment of today's younger population. That was not the case back then. This was a crew cut. This was even less hair than a crew cut. This was strictly a bottom of the barrel, last in the pecking order, you got no friends style of haircut. Well, now my evening's companions had this haircut. They also got a night's free lodging in Remann Hall, Tacoma's teen slammer.

They were out of jail the next day and, for some reason, no formal charges were filed. I was never contacted and my father never mentioned the missing siren. Dick got his car back and the siren likely began residence in some other law enforcement officer's basement. Ricky, despite being temporarily bald, became just a little bit cooler in some of the neighborhood kids' eyes. I earned a little more status for being Ricky's buddy, and for "getting away with it."

Best of all, Ricky's sister began talking to me. Who says that crime doesn't pay?

The Unknown Thingy

There sat our beautiful 1956 Cadillac just waiting to be "borrowed."

At ten years of age I had not yet had my first driving lesson, but, I thought, how hard could it be? You climbed in, turned the key, moved that stick thingy, grabbed hold of the steering wheel, pushed on one of the pushy thingies on the floor and then the Cadillac would do the rest. I'd seen my dad do it lots of times. Even my creepy big sister Judy was driving the Cadillac and I knew that I was much smarter than Judy.

The day arrived for my self-taught driving lesson. I was home alone when I heard the Cadillac whisper to me, "No one will know if you take me for a little drive. No one will notice the baby-faced driver peeking through the steering wheel as he speeds majestically around the neighborhood (I didn't know what majestically meant but it sounded good). You know where the keys are so go ahead and drive me." The Cadillac's steady beckoning was more than I could resist, so out of the house and into the car I went.

OK, it was time to do the things I often watched my dad do to make the car move. I had never seen my sister do any of these things because I was smart enough to never go with her for a ride. I put the key in the keyhole thingy, turned it and, just as I expected, the Cadillac started. I knew I was really smart and this proved it. Now what? My dad always grabbed the stick thingy and pulled on it and the car always began moving. I pulled on the shiny stick thingy but nothing happened. I rocked the steering wheel from side to side and still nothing happened. That's right, I remembered; you also need to push on one of those peddle thingies on the floor. This was going to be great! I pushed a floor thingy and moved the steering wheel but the car didn't move at all, although it did make noises like something was about to happen. I tried to remember what my dad always did and again went through all the steps. The Cadillac groaned a bit but just sat there.

I was frustrated that my first self-taught driving lesson didn't appear to include any driving. I got out of the car, returned the key to my parents' off-limits bedroom, and tried to figure out how my creepy sister could make it go but I, the smartest of the Lambert siblings, couldn't make it move at all.

Later that week I watched my dad very closely as he was

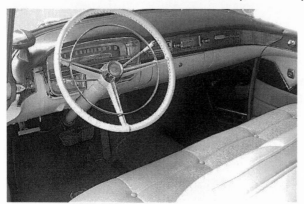

about to start the car and drive the family to church. "Hey, Dad, what does that thingy on the side do?" I asked.

"That's the emergency brake," he said as we pulled away from the curb.

Maybe my sister was smarter than me after all.

Wheels of Justice

I have always had a fascination with police cars, probably due to my father's 20-year career as a police officer in Tacoma. He started as a rookie in 1949 and ended his tenure in 1969 as a detective. I was always so proud to see my dad leaving for work in his uniform that included every gizmo that a police officer needs to fight crime. There was, of course, the gun, handcuffs, billy club and bullets. But the coolest piece of equipment was the police car.

I think my first ride in a police car may have been when I received a hit in the nose during a football game at my grade school. Throughout my academic career I grabbed any opportunity to get out of school, and I realized that, by keeping the blood flowing, I would likely be released from the halls of elementary education. My father was called and he came to my rescue in a gleaming 1957 Ford police car. He came walking down the hall in his uniform for the world and my curious, and perhaps envious, classmates to see. Dad and I left the building, climbed into the police car, and drove off into the afternoon sun looking like, in my eyes, the two most important people in the world.

The next day a few classmates commented about seeing me leaving school in the care of a police officer. I told them that he was my father and they responded as if I was the son of Superman.

One unofficial and unauthorized use for Dad's police car was bill collecting. My brother Jay had a paper route in a part of town where the residents seemed to have difficulty paying their monthly bill. Jay's routine was to walk the route and collect payment once a month. This always resulted in a few customers giving him various reasons for not paying and asking him to come back some other time. He did, in a police car. It was amazing how many customers had no problem finding the money when they saw that he had arrived in a blue sedan with a red gumball dispenser on the roof.

One of my favorite memories was spending an entire day riding with Dad in a city-police-issue 1959 Ford. It was very exciting to observe him as he drove around the city investigating various illegal activities. The two big criminal capers we looked into that day were the theft of a ladder and, I'm not kidding, the theft of a lawn. The short investigation revealed that the person reporting the stolen lawn had not paid the landscaping company for the sod installation, so the company just came back at night, rolled up the lawn, and took it away.

Occasionally Dad would give me a ride to a friend's house, and, despite his reluctance and due to my persistence, I was allowed to announce my arrival by pushing on the horn ring and causing the siren to wail. I'm sure many parents were not very happy to hear my arrival.

REX J. LAMBERT
Detective

TACOMA POLICE DEPARTMENT
County-City Building
Tacoma 2, Washington

FUlton 3-3311
Ext. 294

Not all of my rides in police cars have been warm and fuzzy father-and-son outings; however, every police car I see reminds me of those few wonderful times spent with Officer Lambert.

Oh Chute!

The stories I tell are usually about cars in one form or another. This story is about an un-powered, un-wheeled form of transportation under the control of an unintelligent 13 year old boy.

My father collected an odd assortment of stuff, resulting in my boyhood residence being a combination scrap yard and recycling center. There were piles of used plumbing fixtures, a junk motorcycle, a case of flare gun charges and rolled up sheets of roofing tar paper. There were several discarded workbenches that I turned into a pirate ship, boxes of glass chandelier parts that I pretended were pirate treasure and dozens of gallon jugs that I filled with water and shot with my pirate's musket (slingshot). Amongst the various castoffs was an item that was the best of all--a camouflage green parachute.

This surplus military freight parachute was used for dropping supplies into remote locations so G.I.s could have lots of yummy two-year-old biscuits or whatever items they were short of on the battlefield. It was a bit smaller than what would be used to float a nearly full grown soldier to the ground, making it perfect to float this 13-year-old boy around the neighborhood.

My first foray into the wild blue yonder was at nearby Franklin Park. I reasoned that if I spread out the open parachute on the side of the hill and began running, it would inflate and, well, do something dangerous and exciting. This was long before base jumping, parasailing and other two-digit I.Q. activities became the passion of many thrill-seeking invincible young adults.

So there I was, repeatedly running down the hill with a parachute behind me that occasionally actually filled up, rose above me and transported me up and away from the ground! I floated for distances of a few feet to perhaps fifty feet.

This method of travel worked well for several flights until a takeoff that resulted in the parachute canopy traveling rapidly forward instead of slowly upward. Picture a cartoon where the hapless character's legs are spinning wildly as he attempts to keep up with whatever is forcing him to go faster than nature intends. Put my face on that character and you have a good idea of what was going on in my life at that moment. It all came to an abrupt end when a fence surrounding a tennis court stopped my forward momentum. I was propelled into a metal post that left a lasting impression on my rib cage. To this day I have a section of my ribs that don't reside where the rest of my ribs do.

My flights around the neighborhood continued until the fateful day when I got tangled up in a tree. As I attempted to extract myself, the parachute ripped and I had to put my budding career as a skydiver temporarily on hold.

Fifteen years later I found myself stepping out the door of an airplane that had been doing an excellent job of transporting me and was in no need of exiting. I repeated this mode of travel several times until the day that my parachute decided to not properly open. That was also the day that I retired from my adventures in unpowered transportation.

Losers, Lambrettas and Ladies

I wasn't a hoodlum, but nearly everyone I ran around with was.

My first couple of years at Tacoma's Jason Lee (Chasing Fleas) Junior High School had been spent hanging out with the crowd that every parent hates--the "bad kids." I felt that they were a lot more fun than the "good kids." They were, at least for a while. Then things began to get out of control. In the seventh grade we participated in activities and pranks that ranged from innocent to just a little bad. Perhaps definitions are in order. Innocent: jumping up and down on the rear bumper of grumpy Mr. Bass' 1956 Packard and making the suspension automatically raise the car. Just a little bad: sleeping overnight in a friend's back yard and swiping his parents' 1958 Nash and going for a joy ride. Not too serious stuff. Not yet anyway.

Then something happened in the summer of 1961. My buddies began removing parts off other people's cars rather than fooling around with the suspensions. (Did you know that only one screw holds the entire taillight assembly on a 1959 Cadillac?) Our crowd was now taking joy rides in cars whose owners we didn't know. What was a nice kid like me doing with this crowd of slammer-bound thugs?

I needed help.

I met Dale my first day in kindergarten and we have been good friends ever since. He was one of the "good kids" and, therefore, was not a part of the bad behavior of my immediate crowd. Dale came over one day and said that he wanted to talk to me "man to man." He had observed how things were getting out of hand with my crowd and that I needed to get away from them. He was right. He pointed out how some of my friends were juvenile delinquents who were headed for residence in state institutions. Again he was right. He reminded me that it didn't matter that I was not actually participating in the worst actions of the group. I would likely somehow get caught up in them and end up in jail with the rest of these guys. Yet again he was right. Then he said the magic words-- the words that almost every pubescent boy wants to hear: "I know a couple of girls who like you and think that you are cute." That was the good news. The bad news was that these girls would have nothing to do with me because I hung out with the "wrong crowd." I didn't need to hear any more. This was not a difficult choice: hang out with losers or hang out with a girl or two.

The change was overnight. I mean that literally. The next morning I began dressing differently, combing my hair differently and, most importantly, disassociating myself from the slammer-bound boys. I managed to quickly remove myself from this group; however, I still couldn't seem to get the attention of any of the promised girls. I needed a secret weapon. I needed something that would make me the most irresistible boy in school. Something that would catapult me to the top of the desirable boy list. Something that no girl could resist. I needed a motor scooter!

My dad had recently purchased a brand new 150cc Lambretta motor scooter. No, it was not a fancy convertible or a sexy sports car. What you have to remember is that these girls were 14 or 15 years old and any set of wheels impressed them, even if the set only included two wheels.

Here was my game plan: I would sneak out of school early, swipe Dad's scooter and drive by the school just as the day's classes were ending. I sat parked a block away and waited as my fellow students spilled out onto the school yard and surrounding streets. I started the Lambretta and slowly passed by hundreds of my classmates. Many of them stopped and gaped at the kid on the scooter. I drove down the street, turned around and made another pass through the young crowd. My plan worked perfectly.

The following day classmates that had never spoken to me were now saying hello. Girls smiled at me as I passed down the school's hallways. I was receiving friendly stares rather than hostile glares. I didn't care that this acceptance was based on me having a vehicle. Anything that would open the right doors was OK with me.

Dear old Dad seemed to always look the other way when I would drop by his house (divorced parents, broken home, poor me) and borrow the Lambretta. His being a police officer resulted in other police officers not bothering the scooter-straddling squirt who was obviously too young to be driving.

I gave girls rides after school and I began being invited to parties. "I'm having a party Saturday night and you are invited. Can you bring your scooter?" In a very short period I went from not being acknowledged by girls to having them sitting on the Lambretta with their arms around me and their bodies pressed against me.

Over the next year some significant things happened. A few members of my previous circle of friends ended up going to jail. Old grumpy Mr. Bass, who made his living as a beautician, became my mother's hairdresser. As I got a bit older he began showing up at my house to visit my mother. He'd toss me the keys to his 1955 Buick and tell me to go ahead and take it for a spin. The next thing I knew he was my stepfather. Illegally driving the Buick rather than the Lambretta seemed like a better choice.

I moved on to high school, bought a vehicle with four wheels, and fortunately maintained my place among the "good kids."

I still love Lambretta motor scooters.

My First Car Club

I've had two great passions since I was old enough to push a toy car on the kitchen floor--automobiles and clubs. By the time I was 12 years old I had started the Junior Fireman Club, the Junior G-Man Club, the Back Ally Boys and the Oddballs.

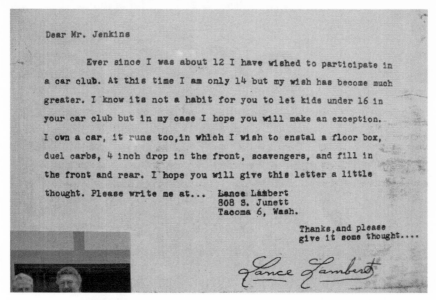

Dear Mr. Jenkins

Ever since I was about 12 I have wished to participate in a car club. At this time I am only 14 but my wish has become much greater. I know its not a habit for you to let kids under 16 in your car club but in my case I hope you will make an exception. I own a car, it runs too, in which I wish to enstal a floor box, duel carbs, 4 inch drop in the front, scavengers, and fill in the front and rear. I hope you will give this letter a little thought. Please write me at... Lance Lambert
808 S. Junett
Tacoma 6, Wash.

Thanks, and please give it some thought....

Lance Lambert

When I was 14 years old I wanted to join the Toppers Car Club. They were the most active and respected club in the town. I was allowed to attend several of their meetings; however, they said I couldn't join until I was 16 years old and had a driver's license. They did offer to help me start the "Junior" Toppers Car Club. I felt that I was beyond the "junior" stage so I decided to start my own club.

Most of my closest friends were into cars as much as I was, so I recruited them to become charter members. There were six of us, aged 15 and 16, with two members owning cars. Bob Dillon had a 1947 Hudson and Greg Eling had a 1940 Chevrolet. It was the summer of 1962 and there we were, Greg Eling, Bob Dillon, Jim Johnson, Doug Sparks, Dale Query and myself, sitting in my parent's garage. First of all we had to come up with a name for the club. I picked up an old copy of "Ivanhoe" and started glancing at the pages to see if anything jumped out at me. I saw the word *steeds* and that was it! Steeds equaled horsepower and strength. It was perfect. We

agreed on the name and began the next steps in organizing a club--designing the club's emblem, car club plaques and the club membership card. It soon became apparent that a better club name could have been chosen. People occasionally asked, "Steve's car club? Who's Steve?" Or, "Why a horse? Is this a 4H club?" In later years people asked if we were a Mustang club.

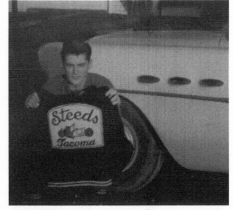

Our first emblem featured a T-bucket hot rod but we quickly changed that to a more fitting horse's head and engine combination.

We quickly overcame any name-related problems and become one of the largest and most active car clubs in town. We had great looking club jackets, several car-show-winning vehicles, a club dragster (later destroyed when it flew off the trailer and crashed into the tow truck), and membership in the Northwest Car Club Council and the International Car Club Association. At any given time there were usually about 15 active members in the club.

The members' cars ranged from beater four-door sedans to a new Corvette. Some members, like me, were happy with cars that would get them reliably from home to the local drive-in and back again. Others were only content when they felt their car was the fastest on the boulevard. My contributions to the club's roster were a mildly customized two-door 1948 Chevrolet Fleetline and a lowered and rumbling 1954 Oldsmobile 88 two-door hardtop. The Fleetline had a lowered front end and a partially rolled and pleated interior. The Olds was lowered

three inches and had a leaded-in trunk lid. Of course, each car proudly displayed the club plaque in the rear window.

The majority of my attention during my high school years was divided between the club and my girlfriend. I couldn't wait for the next kiss from Kayleen or the next weekly club meeting. She often accused me of caring more for the club and my car than I did for her. I was smart enough to change the subject when it came up.

I graduated from high school and prepared to travel to Hawaii to attend college. I reluctantly had to sell my car and my club jacket before I left town.

When I returned home I was pleased to find that the club was still very active, but there were two problems. One was that the membership was a bunch of younger guys I didn't know. Another was that they didn't seem to be impressed that I was one of the original members. But then, it didn't really matter because I'd moved to Seattle and had begun my VW-driving hippy days. The times were changing.

Pizza Sauce and 30-Weight Oil

My first experiences working on cars were during my years of being a pest while my big brother Jay was working on his 1933 Buick, 1939 and 1948 Fords and 1949 Chevrolet. He would give me some simple job, with the results usually leaving me either burned or bleeding. With this confidence-building training I became ready for my own car.

My first car was a 1948 Chevrolet Fleetline (the 24 hour ownership of a 1949 Dodge doesn't count). After one day of owning it I'd gotten my first ticket and after one week of driving it I'd blown up the motor. The next several weeks were spent sitting in the car and pretending that it still ran. I had purchased the car to drive, not to use as a playhouse, so something had to be done.

Jay had made me realize one major thing about working on cars; I didn't enjoy it. Sure, I could hang a muffler, change the oil and other such "no brainers." But I saw the real mechanical work as both a mystery and an unappealing chore.

So there I sat in my Chev pretending to be cruising past my high school and enjoying the admiring glances of my classmates. In reality, the only people who saw me were the neighbors, who likely wondered why the car and its young occupant just sat there.

It was time for action.

My friend Greg Eling, a real mechanic, was replacing the original six-cylinder engine in his 1940 Chevrolet coupe with a Chev 283 V8. What was he going to do with that now-surplus six-cylinder engine? He answered that question by selling it to me for a price that was very easy for him to "stomach." That left me with the chore of putting it into my Fleetline.

Another question was how I could explain to friends at the local hangouts that I had replaced my 1948 engine with the engine from a 1940 Chev? That seemed to be going backwards, against all that was held holy by any young hot rodder.

I had a friend who removed the V8 engine from his 1955 Ford and replaced it with a six-cylinder engine out of a school bus. He was going to be the only guy on the planet who would be lower in the hot rodder pecking order than me. I came up with an answer! I told everyone that my "new" motor was out of a 1949 Chevrolet. That would be acceptable by our stringent standards, so the problem was solved. The fact that all of our mutual friends knew that the motor from Greg's car was being transplanted into my car didn't seem to enter my mind. Research shows that a 16-year-old brain is not fully formed. I was proof of that theory.

Now the big problem: how to join Greg's old engine and my Chev body in holy matrimony? It was time for me to reach deep into my bag of tricks and solve the problem. I had a secret weapon--a weapon that none of my non-mechanically challenged buddies could resist. I had at my disposal a weapon that was so powerful that it was second only to the allure of attention from pubescent females. I had pizza!

I had been working at the local pizza restaurant for several months, and most of the local teenagers were crazy about pizza. During my short tenure, the manager and I had come to an agreement. He was a hardcore alcoholic who wanted to spend as

much time as possible across the street at the local tavern. I worked three weekday evenings and Saturdays. During that time he would cross the street for a refueling that would take the entire evening, leaving me in charge of running the joint. He wouldn't even return to close the restaurant. He gave me the title of assistant manager, but my wage remained at $1.25 per hour. I got the title so that the staff would do what this 16-year-old kid told them to do. But here was the real payoff: he always "looked the other way" when it came to my form of food distribution. I traded pizza for beer. I traded pizza for car parts. I traded pizza for the use of the hoist and tools at the local Union 76 gas station where a friend worked. I fed pizza to a destitute 16-year-old friend who lived on his own. I brought pizza home to my family. And I traded Greg a pizza for his old engine. This monetary system worked great and it also resulted in that little six-cylinder engine being installed in my Chev and a pepperoni pizza being installed in Greg's stomach.

Yes, it was stealing from the company, and, looking back, I feel a bit guilty about it. I convinced myself at the time that, given all of the circumstances, it was an acceptable way to make up for my

lack of a raise for running the place, and also for not "ratting out" my boss.

I told my buddies Greg, Doug, Bob and Darrol that they could have as much free pizza as they wanted,  whenever that wanted it if they would install Greg's surplus engine in my car and get it running properly. I said that I would help, but it was up to them to do the majority of the real work. What would have likely taken me weeks to do took them only one weekend to complete.

I have proof that I actually got my hands dirty while helping with the installation. My mother took a picture of us while we were doing the transplant. I was under the car at the time and gave her a smile. Fortunately she did not take a photo at other times when I fell asleep while under the car. Not just relaxing; I was sound asleep. The rest of the group didn't even notice and they did an excellent job of doing my work for me. By the end of the weekend the car ran great and I had gotten some much-needed sleep.

Now it was time for me to "pay" my mechanics. Those guys could put away pizza and they were "paid" handsomely for their time and talents. I worked at the restaurant for about 18 months, and during that time they came in frequently to receive their pay.

The whole pizza thing was just getting started in Tacoma in 1963, and where I worked was one of the first pizza parlors in town. It was always very busy and crowded with my friends. A few of these friends had 30-weight oil and pizza sauce on their hands. That was OK, because they didn't need to reach into their pockets for money.

Out of Odor

Donna was nice but her feet smelled horrible.

It was March 8, 1963 and it was time for me to buy a car. I'd been 16 years old for nearly 24 hours and that was a long enough wait before I purchased my first "real" car. My stepdad and I went to look at a canary yellow 1948 Chevrolet Fleetline Areosedan that seemed to be in reasonable condition. I'd saved up $125 from my paper route and that's what the seller accepted for the car.

OK, a car is now in my life and it is time to obtain another important thing in a 16-year-old's life--a date. Everyone seemed to think that Donna was the perfect girl for me. She was nice, quick to laugh and attractive. I gave my friends' suggestion some thought and set my sights on Donna.

Having a car my sophomore year elevated me to being one of the "big men on campus" status holders, and therefore, date worthy. I'd made my Chev even cooler by adding 1957 Buick hubcaps and lowering the front end three inches. I was sure that I now owned a car that was irresistible to all of my female classmates.

I worked up my courage and asked Donna if she would like to join me for a few hours at the Auto-View Drive-In Theater. She apparently found my hubcaps irresistible and agreed to spend a Saturday night parked with me in row number 10 at the drive-in.

We were having a great time and really hitting it off well when, for whatever reason, we began tickling each other. Now don't jump to conclusions; I was a nice boy and my intentions were honorable and she was a perfect young lady. Perfect except for her feet. The tickling fest expanded to my reaching down and removing her shoes. OH MY GAWD! Those shoes were magic because they had managed to conceal her horrible foot odor up to this point in the evening. I thought I was going to pass out due to the horrific smell.

Back then every car person had heard the urban legend about the perfect 1958 Corvette that can be bought for only $50 because someone died in it and the smell can't be removed. I'd have sold my Chev for less than that if I'd thought that Donna's foot smell wouldn't go away. I had to get out of the car immediately. I made the

 excuse that I was going to get us something from the refreshment stand so I could get away from her feet as quickly as my own feet would carry me. Now what was I going to do? She put on her shoes before I returned, and the smell had dissipated to the point that I could drive her home. Of course the windows were rolled down.

I probably should have assumed that her feet were having some kind of reaction to my irresistible hubcaps and that this was a hygiene disaster that would not likely happen again. However, I just could not take the chance that this upholstery-melting event might repeat itself. There was no second date, but we did remain friends through high school. She probably told the story many times about the night she went out with some guy who owned the smelliest car in school.

The Hole Story

I spent a lot of time during my high school on activities connected with my membership in the Steeds Car Club. The members, mainly students at Tacoma's Stadium and Wilson High Schools, drove the usual desirable and affordable cars of the time--'40s and '50s Ford and General Motors products. These cars, being affordable, were frequently in need of repairs, so the Steeds membership decided that a place was needed where we could work on our cars. The treasury was raided and a "clubhouse" garage was rented. It was a spacious two-car structure that looked like it should have been located on the main street of Sheriff Taylor's and Barney Fife's Mayberry.

There were two interesting aspects to the garage; it was in rough shape and needed a lot of repairs, and the owner was also in rough shape and needed some repairs, at least in the mental area. One of his charming attributes was the choice of collecting the rent while wearing only a T-shirt. Yes, nothing else, just a raggedy old T-shirt. We drew straws to see which of us had to knock on his door and hand him the $25 monthly rent. It's been almost 45 years and I still can't get that image out of my head.

Among the many repairs the garage needed was of the floor. The concrete was broken and missing in several areas and we felt it reflected poorly on the club's status. We, however, had no idea of how to correctly repair the floor. Filling holes with dirt and gravel was only temporary and created a bit of a mess.

Then came a stroke of luck. A nearby street was being resurfaced with asphalt and, as a result, there was a large pile of fresh asphalt left behind after the workers had quit for the day. The pile was still very hot, and it smoldered as it slowly cooled. So here's how it looked to us: we had a garage with holes in the floor, a nearby street was having its holes filled and there was some surplus (we hoped) asphalt just waiting to be utilized. The solution to our problem was before us!

As night fell we commandeered a wheelbarrow from our nearly naked landlord and began the transfer of the asphalt. We made several trips, and the pile diminished as the garage's holes were filled. Then we raided a member's garage to get a barrel that, when filled with water, was of sufficient weight to roll over the asphalt and compress it into the holes. A nearby garage (my dad's) contained a block of hardened tar that, when melted, provided us with the edging goop that sealed the asphalt to its concrete neighbor. We worked late into the night to finish our asphalt assignment.

The following morning the garage was occupied by several prideful Steeds who had accomplished their common goal--fill the holes and spruce up the clubhouse.

I'm not sure if we stole the asphalt or did the paving crew a favor by getting rid of a pile of surplus asphalt. Any concerned reader should keep in mind that we were young, irresponsible, resourceful and poor in both finances and wisdom.

After a few months we located a better garage and moved out of the "Mayberry" clubhouse. Was the landlord sad to see us leave? I think we just disappeared rather than knock on his door and again be exposed to his exposure.

Good choice.

Dave

Dave was a nutty guy. He was also tough guy. He was not mean, but he definitely never shied away from a physical confrontation. Nobody challenged this guy. When you saw him coming you avoided eye contact and faded into the nearby landscaping. He was feared by everyone in the neighborhood.

Despite this, I somehow managed to become good friends with Dave. I likely cultivated this friendship out of the will to survive, but I quickly realized that Dave was a good guy. He was a little nuts, but a good guy. He would do crazy things like ride his bicycle into the side of a building just to get a laugh. He seemed to have no fear, but this lack of fear was usually motivated by a desire to make his friends laugh. Being his friend and laughing with him was much better than being his enemy and fearing him.

Dave and I began to hang out together during our early teen years. We'd go to his house after school to watch *American Bandstand* and the *Stan Boreson Show*. Then off we'd go on our bikes to cruise the neighborhood and local parks. On weekends we'd work on model cars together. Our successfully built models were displayed in our bedrooms and our less-than-successful models occasionally met their demise via a firecracker or a can of lighter fluid. On more than one occasion Dave painted an entire model (tires, chrome and all) with the closest paint within reach. Flat black or fluorescent colors were his favorites. Then he'd take it out to the back yard and sacrifice it to any God of Fire that might be in the area. He looked a bit frightening when he was squirting lighter fluid on the model while laughing. Yes, Dave was a little nutty.

A few years of friendship went by and then the biggest thing in our lives happened: we turned 16 and got our driver's licenses. Into the closet went our models, replaced by cars in our driveways. Mine was a canary yellow 1948 Chevrolet Fleetline Areo two-door sedan. Dave's car was a pumpkin colored 1956 Renault Dauphine four--door sedan. How did Dave expect to maintain his hard won image as a tough guy while driving a four-door pumpkin colored Renault? How did he ever expect to receive the respect of his peers while driving a French cartoon car? How could he do this to himself? He told me, "I'm tired of being a tough guy and I don't care what anyone thinks about my car." I think the low purchase price was also a factor in his decision.

He started putting his fighting energy into auto antics with that Renault. He could make the car go up incredibly steep wooded slopes while, at the same time, running down various types of vegetation that were nearly as large as the car. He once, just for the fun of doing it, rolled the car over on its top. He would lend it to any friend, even when he knew the guy was going to beat the pudding out of it. He once filled it with beer cans and bottles after a party just because he wanted to see his friends' reactions when they saw the mess in his car.

Once we were at a party when Dave decided to try to make a new friend of a young lady he didn't know. He offered to take her for a ride in his car and she replied, "Bite my ass." He quickly got behind her, dropped to his knees and did exactly what she had suggested. He bit her ass. These days that action might result in Dave being thrown in jail. Back then it resulted in Dave becoming a legend amongst the guys in his hometown.

My next car after the Chev was a 1954 Oldsmobile 88. Dave and I decided to go skiing and strapped our borrowed skis to the roof of the Olds. It was Dave's first time on skis, but this did not deter him from thinking that the sport of skiing would come easily to him. He decided the best way to learn to ski was to go to the Crystal Mountain resort (a challenging slope near Mt. Rainier in Washington State) and attempt to ski down its highest and most difficult run. I strongly advised him against this method of learning to ski. He protested and climbed on the chair lift. This was also his first time getting on and off a chair lift. He went up but I chose not to because I was a lousy skier and would never make it down that slope in one piece.

Dave arrived at the top, surveyed the ski run ahead of him and headed down the slope. Within seconds Dave tumbled out of control and broke his leg. He completed the rest of the run strapped to a board while assisted by two members of the Ski Patrol. The first aid station put a splint on his leg and helped me stuff him into the Oldsmobile. Off to the hospital we drove while Dave made jokes about the entire event.

During an art class in high school my girlfriend was being harassed by a fellow classmate. I hesitated in stopping this action, so Dave took it upon himself to respond to the situation. He followed the guy into the art class supply closet and administered a brief but effective beating. Problem solved.

Unfortunately, my memories of Dave are all from the distant past. Several years ago I was in Washington D.C. and stopped by the Vietnam War Memorial to get a rubbing of Dave's name.

I always smile on the rare occasions that I spot a Renault Dauphine.

Rocket in the Road

Friends and acquaintances assume, since I make my living writing about old cars and producing TV programming about old cars, that I'm knowledgeable about the repair and upkeep of old cars. Believe me, that assumption is wrong.

Many decades ago I was the proud owner of a very nice 1954 Oldsmobile Rocket 88 two-door hardtop. It was black, lowered three inches and shod with reversed wheels. For readers not versed in old car "coolness," lowering a car makes it look better and ride worse, and adding reversed wheels makes the car look better but destroys wheel bearings. Perhaps an appropriate analogy is when women, and some men, wear high heels. It looks great but is bad for your health.

So there I was, driving along Tacoma's 6th Avenue, the main cruising street for all of T town's north end young road devils. The three-and-a-half-mile asphalt and concrete strip was home to several traditional 60s style drive-in restaurants, including Frisko Freeze, Busch's and King's. I guess back then they were just drive-ins, since it was the 1960s when I had this experience. The endless cruising started at Frisko Freeze, at the east end of "The Ave," and ended, or rather provided the turnaround spot for the return trip, at King's Drive-In, located very close to the Narrows Bridge, also known as the "Galloping Gertie" of collapsing suspension bridge fame.

It was a warm summer afternoon and along for the ride was

my good friend Darrol, another car crazy teenager from the ranks of Tacoma's less-than-stellar youth. All was well until the Oldsmobile indicated it was time to replenish the fuel system. The local Shell station came into view and I signaled my intended turn into the lot when suddenly the black beauty decided that it was not going anywhere. It made all of the appropriate noise when the gas pedal was pressed but it just sat there thundering, thanks to the well worn exhaust system.

As stated earlier, my mechanical expertise is a bit lacking. It was obvious to me which end of the car housed the engine and where the hole was located to pour the gas into, but beyond that I was at a loss. Darrol, thankfully being a bit of a stout and sturdy fellow, helped me push the gazillion-pound Detroit-built carcass into the gas station. From out of the garage sauntered the on-duty mechanic who asked if he could be of assistance. This was back when service stations were not just a place to buy three gallons of gas for under a buck. They also had people there who worked on cars rather than just selling you beef jerky and a 62-ounce "cup" of soda.

Usually, mechanics of that era were scruffy guys named Earl who had the ability to diagnose any automotive malady just by the sound of the motor. I was confident that this particular Earl was not going to let me down. He listened intently to my description of the Oldsmobile's dilemma and then rendered his verdict. "It might not be operating properly due to the fact that your driveline is lying out in the street."

Yes, just as he had stated, there in the middle of one of the most traveled thoroughfares in town was my car's former driveline. The driveline, in case you've forgotten, or never knew, is a long metal tube that connects the transmission to the rear wheels and causes the car to move forward, backwards or sideways if you've overestimated your driving skill.

Earl diagnosed the cause of the problem to be either a worn U-joint (don't ask) or the result of excess exuberance by the car's owner when accelerating. My guess is that it was a combination of both theories.

We pushed the broken chariot into the garage where Earl began doing things that, to this day, seem very mysterious to me. It turned out to be an easy fix and Darrol and I were quickly able to return to the goal of the evening--arriving at each of the drive-ins in the grand manner that only a couple of mechanically deficient 17-year-old kids can accomplish.

Beer Bowl 500

It was late on a Saturday evening in 1964, the stadium was empty and Sandy's go-kart was the only vehicle on the track. It was a perfect evening for teenage boys to create a memory.

Sandy was the type of guy everybody loved. He was funny, friendly, generous, supportive and always there when a friend needed a friend. His unique living situation also added to his appeal. His family owned, operated and lived in a very small neighborhood grocery store. It was a charming building resembling something you'd expect to see in a Norman Rockwell painting.

Sandy, like all of his close friends, was nuts about anything with a motor and wheels. The store's basement held a huge slot car track built by Sandy and his friends. Every horizontal surface in his bedroom was covered with greasy used car parts and even his bed didn't escape the horizontal hosting of parts. He used one half of the bed to store car parts and the other half for sleeping.

Sandy's collection of cars, or at least the remnants of cars, consisted of a 1948 Plymouth, a 1949 Chevrolet with a collapsed roof, a 1953 Packard and a 1957 Chevrolet. None of these cars held our interest on this particular summer's evening. What did was his go-kart. In our crowd owning a go-kart was equal to owning the most

desirable toy available on the face of the earth. The difficult part was where to safely drive the go-kart.

Tacoma's Stadium High School (also known as "The Castle" due to its architectural design), was our academic prison during the school year. It was located exactly one block away from Sandy's home. Immediately north of the school was a large sports stadium known as the Stadium Bowl. The Stadium Bowl was just that, a huge subterranean bowl where sporting and civic events had been held regularly since 1910. Fortunately on this particular summer evening it was unused and empty with the exception of Sandy, Bob, Darrol and me. Off to the bowl we went with the go-kart and several recently procured beers. We were all 17 years old and, therefore, an evening of sharing beers and driving the go-kart promised to be both a memorable and an illegal event. Technically we were committing a few crimes, but drinking a beer and driving the go-kart around the bowl seemed quite innocent.

The "Beer Bowl 500" race drivers were the best of friends. We had begun hanging out together while attending Jason Lee Junior High School and had originally become friends because of our shared love of cars. In junior high Sandy was an excellent artist and drew pictures of cars for his friends. Bob was my first close friend to get a driver's license and was the proud owner of a 1947 Hudson. Darrol was good with a wrench and had cool older brothers with cool older cars. I was...well, I really liked cars. When we went on to attend Stadium High School we all became members of the Steeds Car Club, a group of about 15 likeminded teenage car nuts. By then we all owned cars, but go-karts were still very desirable and a bit exotic.

The first noticeable thing about the spring evening's event was the noise. Sandy's go-kart did not have a muffler and was very loud. Releasing the exhaust explosions in the large concrete bowl resulted in the noise being extremely intensified. It sounded fantastic. We were sure that the neighborhood's residents were likely phoning the police and that soon we would be visited by the local authorities. Strangely we didn't care and luckily it didn't happen.

Next to the bowl was a tennis court that we used as our pit stop. The system was simple; we each slowly sipped our beers and waited our turn to blast around the dirt track at breathtaking speeds reaching nearly two digits. The track surrounded the football field so a couple of laps felt like a short but gratifying race. Then it was back to the "pits" to switch drivers and resume sipping on the slowly warming beer.

Yes, we were trespassing, drinking beer and disturbing the neighborhood's peace. We were also creating a cherished teenage memory while doing no real harm. The evening passed, the beer was gone and it was time to return the go-kart to Sandy's garage.

At the end of our senior year I signed Sandy, Bob and Darrol's yearbooks in a significant way: The yearbook contained a photo of the Stadium Bowl and on it I drew a little beer bottle with my name next to it.

Twinkling Teeth and Taped Terror

Duane and I have been good friends for nearly 50 years. One of the reasons that this friendship has endured is because we've done so many crazy things together over the years. We've partied together, traveled Europe together, helped each other through some trying times and, best of all, shared many fun and unusual adventures. A few of our adventures involved Duane's cars, including a very nice 1957 Austin Healey.

A daily activity in our town was cruising along the infamous 6th Avenue in search of friends and fun. The fun part usually consisted of doing something a bit silly or goofy as we drove between our favorite hangouts searching for friends. On these drives we were always willing to try anything new and outlandish.

One evening we decided to do something very different.

Many of my friends and I built model cars and we used "grain of wheat" light bulbs to make the headlights in the models light up. These were very tiny wheat grain sized bulbs connected to two very tiny wires. The wires were so thin that they could be routed through areas of a model car and, happily for me, also thin enough to be inserted between my teeth.

I took 10 of these bulbs and ran the wires so each bulb was between a couple of teeth. I bundled all of the wires together and ran them from the corner of my mouth to a battery in my shirt pocket. The result of all of this high tech engineering was a radiant smile. When I grinned, my mouth was full of little lights shining between my pearly whites.

This electrical engineering feat worked better than we imagined, so we decided that it needed to be shared with friends and strangers. We drove Duane's Austin Healey to Frisko Freeze, a popular local drive-in, and began mingling among the patrons in the always crowded parking lot. I walked up to people and flashed a wide smile. The lighting arrangement worked really well and looked like there was a Christmas tree in my mouth. We, once again, were a big hit with the guys and an oddity to the girls.

Another Austin Healy adventure with Duane was when we used our creativity to turn me into a monster.

We took a roll of masking tape and covered my face with strips of tape. Only my eyes and mouth were exposed and the result was something akin to Frankenstein's monster being turned into a mummy.

It was a beautiful Saturday afternoon that was made for cruising, so we jumped into Duane's car and drove along "The Ave." We'd pull up next to a car and I'd turn and look at the people in the adjoining vehicle. They would immediately look away. I'm not sure if they thought I'd undergone some major injury or if I was just a weird guy in the car next to them. They appeared to not want anything to do with whatever was looking at them from the little sports car.

Later, we stopped by our friend Bob's house to display our creative talents. Another good friend, Toby, was also visiting Bob. I

 jumped out of the Austin Healy and threw Toby over my shoulder. He played dead as we stumbled up and down the street like something from a bad 1950s horror movie. It was a thing of beauty that would have been the envy of Boris Karloff.

Duane, Toby and I are still very close friends. We get together frequently and re-tell stories about our adventures from many decades ago. Occasionally we re-tell the wheat bulb teeth and taped face stories, and we laugh just as hard every time we recall our creative mischief.

I'm still building model cars and I still have some of those bulbs. I wonder…

Corvette Miracle

It was the summer of 1964 and a miracle was about to happen.

The Steeds Car Club had been in existence for more than two years and all was going well. We had about 15 active members, we were one of the best car clubs in Tacoma, and the membership included some great guys with great cars.

What we didn't have was a member with a Corvette.

I always watched for prospective members among the local hot-rod community and found that most guys were eager to join the club. But what I hadn't found was a guy who owned Chevrolet's finest. Car guys now in high school may not know what a Corvette meant to a car guy in 1964; there was no more prestigious car to own than a "Vette." When one drove by you stopped whatever you were doing and just watched the car until it dissolved into a speck on the horizon. Just sitting in a Corvette was better than driving most cars.

Then it happened; somebody with a Corvette expressed interest in coming to a Steeds Car Club meeting. This was not some greaser kid from the neighborhood who drove a fifty-dollar beater. This was a well known guy with a much admired car. Byron melted girls' hearts whenever he walked down the hall at school and filled the guys with envy whenever they saw him driving his Corvette. And, miracle of miracles, he wanted to attend a Steeds meeting.

I was the current club president and wanted to make sure that we made the right impression on Byron. I called most of the members and asked them to be sure to attend the next meeting and to be on their best behavior. I told everyone to treat him normally and not any differently than any other guy, even though he was obviously, due to owning a Corvette, a better human being than any of us.

The next meeting found us standing around and waiting for the arrival of every teenage boy's fantasy. Byron drove up in his 1964

Corvette Stingray and was greeted with nods of approval and an official welcome from the club's president. After the meeting ended we all filed out to kick tires and show off whatever we had done to

 our cars since the previous week's meeting. Then it happened; Byron said he would like to join the club. This was big! This was like, well, having a guy with a Corvette say he wanted to hang out with you. The only thing bigger would be a girl with a Corvette saying she wanted to hang out with you. That thought was so exciting that I can't expound on what effect that would have had on me.

The next meeting arrived and Byron was unanimously voted in as a member. He went on to be one of the club's best members and eventually became its president.

Nineteen-sixty-three Corvettes still raise my pulse rate, and I think of Byron and his Stingray whenever I hear the rumble of a '60s Corvette.

Rebecca's Run

One sunny Saturday afternoon my friends Sandy, Bob, Darrol and I decided to attempt to convince several young ladies that we were the popular vocal group known as Jay and the Americans.

Jay and the Americans recorded 21 singles and 19 albums from 1962 to 1971. Ten of their singles placed in the Top Ten of the Billboard charts and their biggest hit, "Come A Little Bit Closer," released in 1964, made it to the number three spot on Billboard's national chart. They were one of the most successful groups of that era.

The year was 1964 and the place was Tacoma's University of Puget Sound field house. The fans and groupies were excitedly waiting for the arrival of Jay and the Americans, who were scheduled to play a concert that evening. The adoring fans were crowded around the huge back door of the field house hoping that they might get a peek  at their favorite Americans and, perhaps, even get an autograph. Sandy, Bob, Darrol and I decided that we would try to pass ourselves off as the group. The fact that we looked nothing like them and were significantly younger didn't matter to us.

We had two things going for us that might help convince the ladies that we were the real group--a flashy 1963 Thunderbird convertible and Sandy. The T-Bird, borrowed from my stepfather, was good because it seemed like the type of car that one of, or the entire group might arrive in. Sandy was good because, like the members of the group, his hair was just a little bit long. Jay and the Americans were not part of the rising tide of Beatles lookalike groups and instead had much more of the New York City doo-wop group look. Sandy's slightly long hair looked perfect.

We devised a plan to utilize our two advantages. We left the top up on the T-Bird, put Sandy in the back seat, and slowly drove across the field house parking lot towards the gaggle of groupies. I approached within 50 feet of the girls and gave the impression that we wanted to park and go into the building. We slowed down, looked at the fans and then acted like we were afraid they would mob us. Just then Sandy leaned forward and looked out the window. Our plan worked perfectly. The girls started running to the car and yelling out, "Jay! Jay!" I sped up the T-Bird and made a big circle around the parking lot in preparation for repeating our celebrity impersonation. The closer we approached, the more excited the girls became. As we neared them for a second time they again charged the car and began tapping on the windows and yelling for us to stop.

I suddenly felt like I had just arrived at Shea Stadium and was about to have my clothes ripped off by crazed fans. Even worse was the possibility that the T-Bird was about to have its convertible top ripped off. It was time to end the ruse and vacate the premises.

At that moment I realized that the person yelling at my window was my high school classmate Rebecca. At the same moment, she recognized me and figured out that the Thunderbird didn't contain Jay or any of the Americans. She suddenly looked very angry and stopped trotting alongside of the car.

Why were Rebecca and the others so easily fooled? Up close we didn't look anything like Jay and the Americans. Were these girls' nuts? Were we nuts for spending a sunny summer afternoon pretending to be members of a group of which we were not even fans? The answer is likely yes to both questions.

On the positive side, our deception taught us how it felt to be mobbed by adoring fans, and we had a taste of what it was like to be rock stars. But I have to admit that I will never forget the look of disappointment, frustration and anger on Rebecca's face.

Perhaps I'll apologize to her at our next high school reunion.

Confessions of a Car Thief

Many decades ago I was employed as a car parking valet at a fancy-pants restaurant in Tacoma. I'm not going to name the eatery since they, being a place I still can't afford to frequent, likely have good legal counsel and may sue the pants off of me, fancy or not, if they deem this story to be unflattering to their establishment.

At 18 years-old I was trying to gather enough cash to continue my education. At the restaurant I was provided with the opportunity to drive cars that I couldn't afford to own and eat food that I couldn't afford to buy. I could not believe my good fortune at being offered a job that provided both! My wage was simple: keep the tips received from the patrons and order anything from the menu. No paycheck was provided, but it seemed like a fair deal to me. It's likely that my short tenure as a valet resulted in a severe shortage of beef cattle in the State of Washington.

Here was the routine: you the customer drove up in your car, I opened the door for you and your companion, you handed over the keys and entered the restaurant while trying to convince yourself that your cherished chariot had been left in good hands. So far so good, unless you arrived in anything with a convertible top, or a fiberglass body, or was made in Europe, or with a high performance V8, or anything else that flipped my switch. Your car was safe if it was a boring family car that resembled anything my and Millie would drive. But remember, this place was Tacoma's finest eatery and Millie could not afford to dine there. The majority of the clientele drove very desirable cars, not conservative family cars like her Nash.

You arrived and made the mistake of handing your keys to me. Now what? That depends on the car. The usual routine was to park the car in the lot at the front of the restaurant and wait for the next arrival. This was done with the least exciting cars, but the next level up, such as a new Cadillac or Lincoln, were driven across the street to a different parking lot. This gave me a chance to add about a tenth of a mile to the odometer and also experience the acceleration and corning ability of the vehicle. It did no real harm to the diner's car, yet provided this happy valet with a taste of upscale car ownership.

Now for the bad news: beware all owners of Mustangs, Corvettes and all British luxury or sports cars, especially Jaguar

XKEs. Your car was guaranteed to end up in the parking lot across the street, by way of a very scenic route.

The restaurant was located in a remote area that was accessed by a half mile of winding road from the waterfront to the eatery's front door. Off I went to test the car's acceleration and ability to withstand excessive G forces. I drove to the waterfront and then turned around for the rapid return trip to the restaurant. Back I sped, then slowed down and as discreetly as possible parked the car in the lot across from the restaurant. I suppose technically the patron's car had just been stolen, albeit for a short time. Thankfully this perpetrator was never "caught in the act" and asked to explain the indirect parking lot route.

It was part of my job to remember which car belonged to which patron. Upon noticing the car owner preparing to leave the establishment I would have their car waiting in the front driveway. The doors would be open and this smiling valet would hand the keys to the owner with one hand and wait for a tip with the other hand.

My career as an occasional joyriding car thief valet stopped with the end of the summer and the beginning of school. The night that I let a diner's car roll down the restaurant's driveway and crash into another patron's parked car and my boss's car may have also been a factor in my short period of employment.

Enjoy your dining experience tonight. Don't forget to tip the valet.

Manly Mustang

Let me begin by apologizing to my friends in the Mustang community. I assure you that you'll only be upset with me for a short time. Apologies should also be extended to Falcon owners, high school dropouts, women and "manly" men.

The car world was given a friendly slap in the face on April 17, 1964. That was the introduction date of Ford's Mustang, and, as the cliché goes, the rest is history. I, however, was not impressed. To my eyes the design was just a modest Falcon in silk stockings and the car was too "girly." Even Ford referred to it in an early magazine ad as the "Sweetheart of the Supermarket Set." You can't apply current attitudes and sensibilities to the year 1964, and at that time this meant to me that a Mustang was a car for a woman.

The very first Mustang sold in my hometown was driven by a female high school classmate. Sue's ownership added to my perception that the car was not manly enough for a mastodon of manhood such as my 17-year-old self. A 1954 Oldsmobile, weighing nearly two tons, transported me about town and, dang it, that was a real car. It was not some dainty little thing that the Mustang appeared to be in my eyes. Then something, actually two somethings, happened that resulted in my appreciation of the new Mustang-- young love and the threat of violence.

Fred, a classmate and close friend, had been pursuing young Marla, despite the fact that another young man was under the impression that she was already spoken for and that he was the person doing the speaking. This young man, let's call him Vince, was a Stadium High School dropout who looked and acted like all of the dropouts in the old juvenile delinquent movies in the 1950s and 1960s--greasy, slicked-back hair, turned-up collar and a cigarette continuously hanging from his lips. Every high school had at least one student like this walking the halls, or one former student hanging out in the parking lot. Vince was our token greaser and he did a fine job of playing the part.

Vince decided to challenge Fred for Marla's affections. The word spread that the two love-struck competitors were going to fight on Friday night behind the nearby Signal gas station. Fred and his friends arrived at the appropriate time and waited for Vince's arrival. It was a brisk evening, Fred was ready for action and his pals were all there to insure that the fight "was fair" and that neither participant was seriously injured.

Here's where, perhaps, I might begin to win back the favor of you Mustang-loving readers.

In the distance we heard a low rumble that was unmistakably being made by a high-performance car. The sound was followed by the arrival of what, to this day, is one of the most impressive automotive visuals that is stored in my noggin.

Vince drove up in a new 1965 Mustang GT fastback. This dark green rumbling menace slowly emerged from the darkness and pulled up to the crowd. What happened next was not expected; we forgot about the fight and, instead, stood frozen while admiring the car. I'd only seen the fastbacks in magazines but had not yet seen one that could actually be touched. This car was beautiful and, in the context of the situation, a bit fear provoking. The crowd was no longer excitedly anticipating a victory for either opponent. It was mesmerized by the new "fighter" that had entered the ring. The term "muscle car" had not yet been coined but this car definitely enhanced Vince's muscles. The trance was broken and the crowd approached the Mustang to take a closer look. For the moment, Fred was forgotten. Vince sat for a short time staring at Fred while Fred stared back in admiration and, perhaps, fear. Fred had just lost the fight.

Vince knew he'd gotten the best of Fred, so he slipped the Mustang into gear and drove off into the darkness.

Did this event change my opinion of Mustangs? There's one in the garage, two in my past and, hopefully, a few more in my future.

Blissful Idiots

This is going to be a painful story for environmentalists or car lovers to read. At the time of this adventure I was only 19 years old and, like many 19-year-old people, was a blissful idiot. Despite that, the entire incident was a heck of a lot of fun.

One of my crowd's favorite pastimes was to go "brush shaving" in the woods on the outskirts of Tacoma. Brush shaving is when you buy a junker, take it into the woods and proceed to drive over or through as many obstacles as possible. Favorite targets were big bushes or small trees. Hey, it was 1966 and we didn't care much about green things back then.

Keith had just acquired a 1954 Oldsmobile 88 two-door hardtop. Strong pressure and a few beers from his friends convinced him that this car was the next candidate for use in local defoliation. Off Keith and I drove to Bob and Darrol's garage for the proper modifications to the Olds. Following behind was Bob, who must have found the trail we left interesting. Keith and I started to throw out of the windows anything we could unscrew, break or tear off from the interior, all while driving down the street. Out flew radio dials, sun visors, dash knobs, ash trays, rear view mirror, glove box door and anything else we could break loose. Like I said; we were blissful idiots.

Proper preparation included soldering six beer cans to the hood (to look like simulated carburetor stacks) and brazing the doors closed. We didn't want the doors flying open during our jaunt. A pair of floor jack stands were dismantled and used to raise the car's height considerably. A can of fluorescent orange spray paint topped it off with a very striking set of flames on the sides of the car. The Olds was a sight to behold.

The following day was a sunny Saturday and perfect for us to carry out our mission. Six of us split up and climbed into the Oldsmobile and into my 1956 Ford Country Sedan station

wagon. We took the Ford along because of the high probability that the Olds would be meeting its end that day. We crossed the Narrows Bridge heading to an area near the north end of the Tacoma Industrial Airport. This wooded area was new brush shaving territory for us.

We arrived, and Bob climbed into the driver's seat of the doomed hardtop. The rest of us climbed in and off we went. We had only been crashing through the brush for a few minutes when Bob took aim at a small tree. He failed to realize one thing as he bore down on the small tree; it was big enough to hide a large stump behind it. The car was traveling along at 15 or 20 miles an hour, fast enough that the impact was hard and surprising. The front was smashed in and the hood was buckled. We untangled ourselves from each other, realized that no one was hurt, and started laughing uproariously. When the flames started coming out of the engine compartment we stopped laughing and tried getting out; however, the doors being brazed shut was a serious deterrent. Out of the windows we bailed.

Now we wondered what to do. A smashed and burning 1954 Oldsmobile lay before us. I did the only proper thing in this situation. I decided that we needed a bigger fire so I grabbed a tire iron and broke off the gas tank plug, pouring out gas under the car. You guessed it; the gas ignited and we now had a much bigger fire. The trouble was that the surrounding vegetation also began burning. The blissful idiots then realized that perhaps this afternoon's entertainment had gotten out of control. I jumped into the Ford and

headed to the airport to call the fire department. The airport's fire fighters had already spotted the fire and were on the way to put out what they thought was a crashed and burning airplane. We watched them put out the fire as we backed up slowly, climbed into the Ford and made a quick exit.

A few days later the police knocked on Keith's front door. He confirmed that he was the owner of the car. Fortunately the police's main concern seemed to be having the burned-out hulk removed, rather than the apprehension of the brush shaving pyromaniacs. Keith called a junk yard and they took away the remains of the poor old Rocket 88. We heard no more from any authorities. All we were left with was the feeling that maybe a few bad choices had been made, with the worst choice made by me.

It was lucky that we didn't get hurt in the wreck, suffer from burns or start a serious forest fire. We were also lucky that the authorities didn't put us in jail.

Did we learn our lesson? Probably not. A few weeks later we tried to blow up the engine in Bob's 1947 Chrysler.

Fiberglass Fantasy

I had recently graduated from high school and was spending the summer earning money for my approaching career as a college student. College was something that everyone told me was very important. It was where the majority of my friends were headed, and where all the best parties were. There was one problem. I didn't want to go to college. Instead I wanted a Corvette

I had been given the phone number of a guy with a 1956 Corvette for sale. We made arrangements to meet at a nearby bowling alley near my home. The summer afternoon was beautiful, and I was excited.

Down the street came the 'Vette. It was red with a white cove, the top was off, and I was in love. I waved and he pulled up to the curb. I introduced myself and then walked around the fiberglass beauty. Close inspection revealed only two minor flaws: faded upholstery and a cracked steering wheel insert. This car was gorgeous.

I climbed behind the wheel and headed down 6th Avenue, the most heavily traveled arterial in my end of town. This was the cruising street, and I was sure of bragging rights for at least a week if I was spotted by any of my buddies. But not a buddy or even anyone I knew was to be seen. Oh well, I still was in heaven on wheels.

The car drove as well as it looked. It handled great, had plenty of power and felt like an expression of everything good about automobiles and driving. There were a few problems, however. The asking price was $1500, a good price even in 1965 dollars, but I only had $200. My sister Judy would surely lend her darling little brother the necessary funds. She was a school teacher, which meant, in my mind, that she made a lot of money. She must have a lot of excess funds available for such things as helping her youngest sibling begin residency behind the wheel of a Corvette.

Second problem: what about college? My savings of $200 was to be added to the tuition fund. But, hey, owning a Corvette was much more important than continuing my education.

Third problem: There was a war in Southeast Asia, and it was beginning to get very serious. It was serious enough that you had a problem if you were an 18-year-old single guy sitting in a Corvette instead of a college classroom.

So I had to make a decision. Do I buy the Corvette and enjoy being a 6th Avenue God until I receive a brief, attention-getting note from Uncle Sam? Or do I go to college, let someone else get the note, and experience the exaggerated joys of college life? I reluctantly made the wisest choice, thanked the Corvette guy for his time and sadly meandered down the street thinking about the now-unattainable joys of Corvette ownership.

My first attempt at college was brief. I dropped out after six months, got drafted after all, and then flunked the physical due to two previously undetected stomach ulcers.

By then the Corvette was nowhere to be found, which was OK because I was still too poor to buy it. I also learned that my sister's paycheck did not leave enough to indulge her little brother's fiberglass fantasy. I used my own money and settled for a 1959 Rambler, and then got on with my life.

A 1959 Rambler is nothing like a 1956 Corvette.

Dale Did It

In the distant past I've had the distinct and dangerous pleasure of being a motorcycle owner. It all began with a two-wheeled "doodlebug" powered by a two-horsepower Briggs & Stratton lawn mower engine. My first "street legal" double-wheeled delight, albeit not exactly a true motorcycle, was a Lambretta 150 CC motor scooter. Soon it was followed by a more powerful 175 CC Lambretta. My father was the actual owner of these vehicles, but allowed me unlimited use of both.

These now-trendy collectible scooters were not the height of cool back in the early 1960s. However, remember that having any form of powered mobility at the age of 15 was an instant propellant to the heights of 9th grade popularity. At the age of 16 I left the scooters in the garage and purchased a well used vehicle that traveled around on four wheels. All went well until my buddy Dale knocked my world off its axis.

Dale was, and still is, one of my best friends. We met on our first day in Mrs. Plotts' kindergarten class at Franklin Elementary School in Tacoma, WA. Dale introduced himself and helped me through what I still remember as a very traumatic beginning to a less-than-stellar academic career. Dale joined me in many of my life's high points and helped me through a few of the low points. He was the one neighborhood kid about whom my parents would say things like,

"How's Dale? We haven't seen him in a few days. We wish you'd get good grades like Dale does." The two most momentous things Dale did for me were to get me off the road to Hoodlumville, and a few years later, get me back on the road to two-wheeled pleasure.

Visualize this if you will: It's a beautiful sunny day in the summer of 1967 and a few of my buddies and I are sitting on the porch of my house. Off in the distance echoed the unmistakable sound of a Honda 305 Scrambler. These bikes revolutionized the motorcycle world by proving that, despite Britain's best efforts to the contrary, motorcycles could be both affordable and reliable. The Honda's sound grew louder, and up rode Dale on a brand new Scrambler. Honda had managed to design a bike that was both beautiful and looked like a respectable motorcycle should look. At the time the market was flooded with many choices of small output bikes that, unfortunately, looked like nerdy motorcycle wannabees. "Real" bikes were British manufactured Triumphs, BSAs, Nortons and Matchless', or the American gorillas built by Harley Davidson. Japanese manufacturers made many dependable bikes, but they had yet to design one that had strong appeal to the American market.

I grabbed my ever present camera and took a picture of Dale on his new steed. His contemporaries always had him on a varying level pedestal, and on this day that pedestal shot up to a new height. There was only one way to deal with this--go buy a new 305. The local, and only, Honda dealership had a showroom full of these bikes at a very reasonable $775 "out the door" price. This included a helmet that, at a later date, probably saved my life. I digress; my

mother, being of moderately sound mind, refused to co-sign for the purchase of the bike. I consulted with another good friend, Bob, about my financial dilemma. Bob's mom, having raised Bob, and as a result, no longer being of sound mind, agreed to co-sign for the necessary loan. On that day Bob's mom became my new best friend and my mother's public enemy number one.

Out of the showroom I rode along with seven of my buddies on their new 305s. Within a couple of weeks after Dale's two-wheeled arrival, a new motorcycle gang consisting of several of his childhood pals were all riding motorcycles and terrorizing the local streets.

The first thing we all did to our new 305s was take off the mufflers. A sweeter sound will never be heard than that of an un-muffled 305 Scrambler. The second thing to do was to not do a second thing. These bikes were perfect right out of the box with a silver and black paint scheme, graceful and aggressive fenders, and a seat big enough to be comfortable but small enough to force your girlfriend to snuggle up close.

That motorcycle was my only means of transportation, due mostly to pleasure and poverty. The pleasure resulted from the wind in my face and the power at my fingertips. The poverty was from the hefty $35 a month payments. My buddies and I would ride to far-away exotic locations like Portland, OR, and Walla Walla, WA. We even went to a foreign country by crossing our northern border and spending a few days trying to figure out how fast 80 MPH was in kilometers. It wasn't long before my crowd sold off their bikes to finance the purchase of more useful transportation. I chose to step up to a prestigious Triumph 650 Bonneville. That was the beginning of the end of my motorcycle riding career.

Karma Triumph

The sun was out, the road was straight, and my 1960 Triumph Bonneville motorcycle was running perfectly.

I was going up a long stretch in Tacoma that provides the transition from the once-bustling downtown area to the beginning of T town's residential neighborhood. The speed limit was 25 miles per hour, and on that road, on that day, while riding that motorcycle, I turned into what can best be described as an over-zealous law-abiding citizen—but only after I'd first broken the law.

I was accelerating up the hill when I glanced down at my speedometer and realized that I was traveling at more than 80 miles per hour. Common sense, up to this point being totally absent, returned, and upon cresting the hill, I decided to slow down. This was a good decision considering that, much to my surprise, parked several blocks ahead was a radar-equipped police car. At that time the Tacoma police force was utilizing a large radar apparatus that was mounted on the exterior of the driver's side of the car and was quite visible to passing or approaching motorists. There was no getting around the situation that I had sped into; I was a marked man. I'm sure that what happened next provided this officer with a topic of conversation at his next coffee break.

I downshifted the Bonneville, applied the brakes and, upon approaching the officer's vehicle, pulled directly in front of his car. I parked the Triumph and walked up to the officer's window. He was not worried or apprehensive; he was amazed. Not only was he not going to have to chase this small-town Evel Knievel, he wasn't even going to have to get out of his car.

"I've never seen anyone do this before," he said. "I've never heard of anyone doing this before. I'll likely never see anyone do this again." He was dumbfounded that a speeding motorcyclist would not only hit the brakes upon spotting him, but would actually pull over, stop and turn himself in.

Why would I make absolutely sure that I was going to get a ticket?

You won't find anyone who respects police officers more than I do. Day after day they have to deal with life's tragedies, angry and unappreciative citizens, people who don't like them and people who are scared of them. There was no question as to what his purpose was for being parked there and, as a result, a speeding ticket was going to be issued. It was his job to provide me with an experience that, hopefully, would in the future cause me to not travel at more than three times the speed limit. By pulling myself over I showed him respect and, perhaps more importantly, showed him that there were a few citizens, even ones on motorcycles, who would like to see a police officer's day go just a 1 bit easier. I was putting out a little "good karma," which, it turned out, came back to me immediately.

He took my license, checked to make sure that there were no outstanding felony warrants (hey, I watch COPS and I know the jargon) and then, here's the good karma part, wrote a speeding ticket for ten miles over the limit. It stated 35 in a 25, not the actual 80 that I had been traveling when cresting the hill and into the sights of his radar detector. This was several years ago, and the radar equipment didn't permanently record my actual speed; it just let that officer know how fast I was going when the radar system caught me in its beam. For him there would be no "Lucy, you got some 'splaining to do" back at the station. And yes, I know, he was, in some people's opinions, breaking the law by giving this citizen a break; however, his gesture likely expressed his appreciation to me for showing him some respect.

Try it sometime. Not the speeding, just the effort to make some local officer's day a little easier.

Bad Mechanic; Worse Liar

At the age of 19 I was the proud owner of a 1962 Rambler Classic four-door sedan. It was pristine – great body, paint and interior. One problem – it ran terribly.

It ran when I bought it, but in my 19-year-old wisdom I decided to rebuild the engine. The key word here is "I." I, being me, had absolutely no experience in such matters. Oh, I was great at hanging out at my friends' garages and sharing my vast automotive wisdom, but when it came to real hands-on mechanical work I was, well, less than mechanically skilled. My every attempt at fixing cars resulted in compounding whatever problem I was attempting to fix.

I got far enough into the Rambler engine "rebuild" to end up with parts everywhere and an engine that was nearly unfixable. I boxed up all the parts, tossed them into the trunk and back seat (so much for the great interior), called a tow truck, and had the car taken to the cheapest garage I could find. There was a reason that the garage was cheap; they were about as good at fixing cars as I was. They did get it running – barely.

It was time to sell this jewel.

I put an ad in the paper and got a call from a young woman looking for a reliable car. "Yes ma'am, it runs great!" Wait a minute! This was a Titanic sized lie that I told this trusting lady. I decided that I was desperate and had to sell this car, lie or no lie. She came to look at the car and agreed to purchase it.

As she was handing me the money, I heard a little voice telling me what a rotten guy I was. I just couldn't do it. I looked at her and said, "This car runs terribly, and I can't sell it to you." Rather than get mad, she thanked me sincerely and said how grateful she was that I had told her the truth. Granted, I was a bit late with the truth, but it finally came out.

She left me there with a car that was going to be very hard to sell. However, good deeds don't go unrewarded. The next day I got a call from a guy interested in the Rambler. He asked about the condition of the body and interior. I explained that they were in excellent condition but, not wanting to repeat the previous day's experience, told him that the motor was shot and the back seat needed a good cleaning. He told me he also owned a 1962 Rambler and he had just rebuilt the engine. His son had wrecked the car so he was looking for a good body to drop his rebuilt motor into. Hallelujah!

He came by the next day and cautiously drove my old and his new Rambler away.

Things have not changed much; I'm still driving an old Rambler, but this 1958 Rambler American has a rebuilt high performance 327-cubic-inch V8 Chevrolet motor in it that runs great.

El Camino Errand

Some employers love to play tricks on their newest employees. Once upon a time the new guy was me and the trick turned out to be on my new boss.

One of my many jobs in the past was as a go-fer and clean-up kid at an automotive glass and upholstery shop. I would help clean up broken glass in cars, remove windshields, strip out interiors, sweep the floors and do any other menial jobs that needed to be done. It was easy work and it involved cars, so all was well. Best of all, the company had a new 1966 Chevrolet El Camino shop truck. It looked great and was a stylish vehicle to run errands in, even if the errand had all of my co-workers laughing behind my back. Little did they know it was me who was laughing at them.

The company had two branches; one was located in Lakewood, just southwest of Tacoma, and the other was located in downtown Tacoma. On one slow day I was asked to drive from the Lakewood shop to the Tacoma shop to pick up the "glass stretcher." The boss said that this tool could be clamped on one end of a sheet of glass and then pulled to stretch the glass. The other employees listened to him and tried to contain their laughter. "OK," I said, while thinking of the fun time soon to be spent in that new blue El Camino. I could hardly contain my own laughter. Off I went on the supposedly fool's errand.

The drive between the shops was about five miles if the most direct route was taken. The problem with the direct route is that it did not include the city's best cruising street--6th Avenue. This north end strip of asphalt and concrete was where all of my friends chose to drive their cars during the daily sojourns up and down this main drag between the city's east and west ends. The usual tour included stops at Frisko Freeze at the east end, King's Drive-in at the west end, and Busch's Drive-in at the center. "The Freeze" was where my crowd spent their posing time, and that's exactly where the El Camino headed. It was not on the direct route to the Tacoma branch of the glass shop, but I didn't care. What was important was to show "my" new wheels to friends and to hang out for a short time.

Down 6th Avenue I cruised in the El Camino, passing King's and Busch's on the way to Frisko Freeze. It was lunchtime and a few friends were enjoying burgers in the parking lot. They admired the new Chev glass hauler and laughed when I told them about me being so "gullible" as to fall for the glass stretching story. They understood what an easy decision it was to make; stay in the shop and clean up broken glass and bits of worn upholstery, or take an hour to have a burger and cruise in the shop's chariot.

I finished the burger, said goodbye to friends and headed to the downtown shop. They had been tipped off that I was coming to pick up the "glass stretcher" and waited in anticipation of my humiliation. "I'm here to get the glass stretcher. They need it at the Lakewood shop," I said. They gave some excuse why it was not there and sent me back. Off I went to retrace my cruising route back to the other shop which, of course included passing by the triad of drive-ins.

Upon my return, the manager asked what took me so long. With a smirk I said, "Not being sure if there really was such a thing as a glass stretcher, I decided to stop at Frisko Freeze and check with some of my car buddies. They have never heard of such a tool." He then realized that he'd provided me an excuse for a long break at the company's expense.

The glass stretcher was never mentioned again.

Vans and Vanity

I was a big rock and roll star once! Well, not exactly a star but I hung out with a big rock and roll band. Well, not exactly a big rock and roll band but they did have a number-one national hit. Well, not exactly number one nationally but it did make the top ten nationally and number one on the West Coast. And I was their manager. Well, not exactly their manager but their road manager. Well, all right, I was one of their roadies (known as "band boys" back then) for a summer.

It was the summer of 1966 and had just flunked my army physical due to having two stomach ulcers. I was a free man! I had recently dropped out of college, was working only part time at a job from hell and was ripe for an adventure.

Two friends of mine, Sandy and Ron, had recently hit the pinnacle of success in the eyes of nearly every teenager in Tacoma. Ron was singing lead and playing the sax and organ for the Fabulous Wailers (AKA just the Wailers to the locals), a Tacoma group that had reached number one in 1959 with their song, "Tall Cool One." They 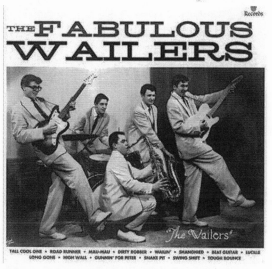 appeared on *American Bandstand* and the *Alan Freed Show* and successfully recorded many albums on local and major labels. During the summer of 1966 they released their latest single, "It's You Alone," which became a regional hit and should have been a national hit. Sandy was their band boy--not the pinnacle of success, but at least a comrade of pinnacle straddlers.

The Wailers were easy to spot: they had a new Ford Econoline van with their name splashed all over the sides, a new Ford Country Squire station wagon with their name splashed all over the sides and a new Oldsmobile sedan with the actual Wailers fabulously splashed all over the inside. It was a real status symbol for a 1960s band to have a van with their name painted on it. It was major status to have a van, station wagon and a big black limousine-style sedan.

One day Sandy and Ron asked me if I would like to go "on the road" with them and the band. This was big! This was like having John Lennon and Paul McCartney ask me if I would like to go along on a world tour with the Beatles. All right, it was nothing like that. But at the time the Fabulous Wailers were the biggest group in Tacoma's music history, for years one of the biggest groups in the Northwest and the biggest thing to ever happen in this boy's 19 years. Included in the offer was a weekly paycheck of $35! That's right, 35 big ones-at least 70 bucks in today's dollars. And all I had to do was unload and load equipment from the van every day, drive from 30 to 300 miles every day, live on no sleep and bad food every day, and cater to every ridiculous Wailer whim every day. That's right; I was being taken advantage of and I loved every day of it!

My duties were varied: I rode in the van with Sandy, usually a few hours or a half a day ahead of the band members. After the show we would pack up the equipment and either head to the hotel or hit the road to the next city. Sometimes I would drive alone in the station wagon to the next town to meet the promoters, get the hotel rooms ready (one room for partying, two rooms for sleeping) and create a little advance publicity for the band. That could be anything from doing an interview on the local radio station to cruising the local hangouts in the station wagon so the fans would see the Wailers painted on the sides and tailgate. It had been years since the Wailers had been number one; however, they were still popular enough to be booked seven nights a week, every week. I traveled with them for three months during which time they had only two nights off. These guys worked very hard and they played very hard.

The venues were everything from broken-down skating rinks to large armories and coliseums. A favorite memory was drag racing the van against another van driven by Chuck, the roadie for the Sonics, another very successful Northwest band. This race was in the Spokane Coliseum. Not AT the Coliseum, but IN the Coliseum where the Wailers were playing a double bill with the Sonics, a common occurrence at that time. The Sonics recorded on the Etiquette label that was owned by the Wailers. It was a short race in which the honor of the Wailers was held high. I didn't even wreck the van. Not this time anyway.

They may have been paying me only $35 a week but I cost them much more. They paid any traffic tickets Sandy or I received. It was amazing how fast a boxy Econoline cold go and it was also amazing how angry some State Patrol officers get when you approached them and did not dim your headlights. They were angry enough to write a ticket.

Did you know that you can make a Ford Econoline with a six cylinder engine do wheel stands? You would think, correctly, that the van would be the least likely "performance" vehicle in the Wailers' stable. And you would think that the van could never do a wheel stand, the result of a vehicle having so much horsepower and torque that, upon accelerating at full power, the front of it rises off of the pavement. But about that you would be wrong.

During that fun summer I learned that by getting as much weight as possible as far back in the van as possible, the rear would go down and the front would go up upon an abrupt departure. So what weighs about 800 pounds and is maneuverable enough to occupy nearly every square inch of the rear couple of feet of the van? Five of the roadie's friends, of course! I only attempted this feat in a safe environment such as a large parking lot full of admiring fans. The image of the band's van, with *The Fabulous Wailers* painted on the sides, traveling a short distance with the front wheels off the ground was a promoter's dream and an insurance company's nightmare.

A serious concern for the band was their ever-increasing insurance premiums. I seemed to have the ability to frequently rearrange the contours of that poor van. I once stopped at a local hangout of the cooler Boise, Idaho crowd to get a burger and promote the evening's concert. I was very cool; I sauntered up to order a burger and nodded appropriately as the crowd gazed in awe at the Wailers' van. I was cool, I was envied, and I was almost a rock and roll star! I returned to the van, put it in reverse and casually backed into a telephone pole. I felt like an idiot as I surveyed the damage, avoided eye contact with the laughing crowd and limped away to face the consequences with my bosses.

You have all heard stories about female groupies, and they are all true. There were always adoring females everywhere the Wailers played. Often they would be waiting when we arrived to set up for a concert or dance. I arrived at the local dance hall in Eureka, California and found a half dozen giggling girls waiting outside of the hall for the band's arrival. Quickly I went into my best rock star imitation. There was a large vacant lot next to the building, allowing me to make a sweeping and graceful approach to the back door of the dance hall. They were all watching, and an evening's companionship for me was assured. My approach was planned as well as any major military campaign. I would drive through the

overgrown vacant lot, cruise directly in front of the girls and give them my shy but fetching rock and roller nod. Then I would park the van and wait for their adoring advances. Everything went great until the first part. The vacant lot was overgrown enough to hide a large piece of abandoned machinery. I don't know what it was but I do know that it was much stronger than a 1966 Ford Econoline. The same Econoline that had just had its body straightened out from my previous drive-in fiasco. Wham! Mr. Rock Star was kissing the windshield instead of an adoring fan. Yes, same idiot, same avoiding eye contact and same angry bosses.

I could only take three months of life on the road, even though the other guys seemed to thrive on it. They gave a great performance every night, partied almost every night but still seemed to maintain their physical and mental health. Not so for me. One morning we were all sitting in a restaurant having breakfast together. I finished my food, went to the restroom, lost a battle with my ulcers, came back to the table and quit my roadie job. It wasn't a hangover; it was just three months of hard working and hard playing. I wished them well and caught a bus home.

I've been on a lot of great adventures in my life and many were about as much fun as a person can have. My summer with the Wailers is near the top of the list. Every day of this roadie adventure provided a now cherished memory. I would have paid them $35 a week for the experience.

Persnickety Paula

Paula was a good friend but a lousy girlfriend.

At the age of 19 I was a struggling student without a job or a place to live. The Army had recently informed me that I was unfit for military duty and my mother had informed me I was unfit for lying-around-the house duty. Where was I to live?

A friend somehow talked her parents into letting me move rent free into an apartment that was built into their garage. Transportation? My dad owned the world's ugliest truck and said that I could borrow it anytime. It was a 1949 International pickup that had formerly belonged to a roofing company. It was beat up and covered with smears of oil and blobs of tar. It was not pretty but it was available.

Paula was also available, but, unlike the truck, she was very pretty. During high school she was a "one of the guys" kind of friend that I never gave any thought to dating. For years it had been me and the guys dropping by Paula's house and eating everything in sight. Her parents loved having us around and her dad was always good for a "when I was your age" story or two.

I'm not sure how it went from me being one of the guys sitting at the kitchen table to me being the kid at the front door dressed in my good jeans, best button down madras shirt and asking Paula if she was ready to go out for the evening. And there, waiting at the curb was that tar-toting truck. Being short on funds meant that our dates consisted of going for rides, hanging out in the parking lot of the local drive-in restaurant, or long walks at Point Defiance Park. Paula thought going to the park was romantic and I thought it was an affordable way to spend time together.

All was going well until our first date when she realized that we would be touring town in the tar truck. She climbed in, but refused to touch anything as she sat with as little of her little bottom touching the seat as possible. I'll admit that a 1949 International truck isn't the height of automotive styling and that tar blobs were not on the options list, but it was transportation, it was free and it was all that I had to drive.

About our third date Paula informed me that she would no longer be riding in the tar truck and that I needed to find a new set of wheels if I wanted to continue our new dating status. I informed her that I had grown tired of her acting like she was entering an outhouse every time she climbed into the pickup. About this time I met another young lady, coincidentally also named Paula, who owned a very nice 1957 Plymouth. It was unlikely that Paula #2 would be willing to chauffeur Paula #1 and me on dates, so something needed to change. Let's see…persnickety Paula or Plymouth Paula. Paula #1 agreed that we made better friends than boyfriend/girlfriend, so we amiably ended our short-lived romance. Time passed and I got a job and purchased a very nice 1959 Volkswagen. Unfortunately, Plymouth Paula turned out to be the girlfriend from hell, so she was also replaced with a better model.

That Was a Close One!

Have you ever had a dozen police officers pointing their guns at you and yelling, "Get out of the car with your hands over your heads?"

I was living south of Seattle at the time, in an apartment that was originally built as a motel and looked like something you frequently see in episodes of "Cops." Back then, as a struggling college student, luxurious accommodations were not in my budget. My buddies Keith and John had stopped by for a visit, and John decided that he wanted to connect with a female friend who lived

nearby. I didn't have a phone, so we jumped in John's 1949 Chevrolet sedan delivery and headed to the nearby Midway Drive-in Theater to use the phone booth that was located at the entrance. John called his friend and she invited him over for

coffee. We headed back to my apartment so John could get rid of us and respond to his friend's invitation.

We pulled into the parking lot of my apartment and were immediately surrounded by police cars. We had no idea what was happening, but we definitely knew that this was no time to make anything that might be interpreted as a "wrong move." There were five police cars and they all had their doors open with the officers crouched down and pointing handguns and shotguns at us. I could hear Elmer Fudd telling Bugs Bunny to "Be careful, be vewy vewy careful."

Keith, John and I usually tried to laugh our way out of any bad situations, but we felt that this was not the appropriate response in this situation. We felt that the officers' funny bones didn't need to be tickled at this moment. We were handcuffed, separated and informed of our rights. To the officers' credit, they were totally professional and treated us with respect as they put each of us in a different patrol car.

We were told that John and his somewhat rare sedan delivery

matched the description of someone who had just robbed the Midway Drive-In Theater. Along with the police officers was the manager of the drive-in who kept yelling "That's the guy, he's the one." What we were soon to find out was that he had not seen the robbery. A teenage girl working in the ticket booth was the person robbed, not this excitable goofball.

We were then taken to the drive-in to be identified by the robbery victim. The police marched us to where the still very shaken young lady was waiting to identify us. I realized that at that moment my life might be about to change from a struggling college student to the new kid in the cell block. The still ranting manager left us for a moment and then returned with the robbery-victim ticket seller so she could take a look at the Dillinger Gang. She was still crying when she looked at John and said, "That's not him."

Several things then happened – I didn't wet my pants, the police visibly relaxed, the manager looked a bit sheepish, and my starving student instincts kicked in. I looked at the manager, and in my best grownup voice said, "I think you should give us some free passes to your theater for putting us through this ordeal." John, Keith and I were each given a book of movie passes with each pass being good for a carload of people and redeemable at several Seattle and Tacoma area drive-in theaters. We were released from the handcuffs and taken back to my apartment by a very friendly and relaxed police officer. He wished us well and drove away.

There the three of us stood, a bit dazed as we realized that we were not going to have to spend the next ten years in jail and the rest of our lives professing our innocence. What we did do was spend a lot of time going to a lot of drive-in movies with a lot of friends stuffed in our cars.

As the cliché' goes, "That was a close one!"

Idiot in the Arterial

There's an old motorcyclist cliché that there are two types of motorcycle riders: those who have crashed and those who will crash. Unfortunately I'm one of the former.

My 1960 Triumph 650 Bonneville was a very cool ride with its sprung chopper front end and high riser handlebars. It was everything decent folk feared and young women admired, or so I thought.

At the time I was stricken with the dreaded social disease egotism, a malady that causes a young man to constantly remind others that the world revolves around him. This disease caused my Triumph to go from a very good looking motorcycle to a not-so-good-looking modern art sculpture. It also illustrated the appropriateness of wearing a crash helmet when riding a motorcycle.

I was driving on a major arterial in my home town when I came upon three attractive young ladies in a 1966 Mustang convertible. The top was down and they seemed to be enjoying the ride. The sun was shining and my Triumph was running as well as any British-built vehicle can; that is to say, it had not broken down yet that day. My egotism suddenly overcame my common sense as I approached the beautiful beauty-filled convertible. I passed the Mustang, looked over at the bevy of beauties and gave them my best "Yes, that's right ladies, this stud on two wheels is your dream come true" look when, much to my dismay, a car in front of me had stopped. Everything went into slow motion as I crashed into the rear of the car. I looked down and watched the motorcycle's handlebar pass under me, followed by the car's trunk, top and hood. It was like I had all the afternoon to enjoy the passing view before I returned my tray to the upright position and buckled my seatbelt. Not so gracefully I made contact with the ground in a perfect three point landing--my head, elbow and knee. My knee injury was minor and only required a large band-aid and a new pair of Levis. My elbow lost the majority of its freckled surface, which, in the following weeks, healed, but, strangely, didn't replace the freckles during the recovery. My head was fine but my helmet was not; it looked like it had been hit with a huge piece of asphalt and at that moment I realized that, in fact, it had been hit with a huge piece of an arterial street. Fortunately, no artery was spilling blood onto the arterial.

As the fog cleared I realized several things: my Triumph was a mess, I was an idiot, and worst of all, the three young ladies, though kind enough to stop and make sure I was OK, were now laughing at this two-wheeled stud lying in the street. It was not the reaction that only moments ago I'd hoped to elicit from them. Not one of the ladies offered me her phone number.

In the following weeks I managed to scrounge up enough money to have the motorcycle fixed. I'm sure the guy who stole it a month later appreciated my efforts.

Suffering From the Benz

It was a pleasant Sunday evening when I met my wife-to-be. I was a shaggy, bearded Grizzly Adams wannabe and Jan was, like now, a tall, thin brunette who looked to me like a cross between Cher and Ali McGraw. This particular evening found us both attending a class being taught at the local Unitarian Church. Actually, she was attending the class; I was just there to meet some wild and crazy Unitarian woman who might like to debate the existence of a superior being while riding around in my 1962 Mercedes Benz.

I had strayed away from my usual path of driving a very old American car to driving something more exotic and, therefore, impossible to find parts for or afford to have repaired. The theory was that the sight of my unshaven and un-sheared head sitting in an oatmeal brown Mercedes was likely to be irresistible to any woman. I had been unsuccessful in proving that theory for a couple of years when I stumbled across Jan that evening.

I created an excuse to strike up a conversation with her and then quickly dropped into our discussion the fact that I drove a Mercedes. She, like the women before her, didn't seem to appreciate the widely known fact that all women find a Mercedes-owning man irresistible. Didn't she know that any unshaven guy driving a 15-year-old, beat-up exotic car was likely a guy on his way up? I assumed that she overlooked the fact that the car was a four-door sedan painted a color resembling a tepid bowl of porridge. Didn't she wonder if the driver might be exotic and desirable in life's many other offerings?

I procured her phone number, and within a week fate had us riding together in the Quaker-Oats-colored chariot. Two things happened as the relationship progressed; she got even better and the Mercedes got even worse. Jan was always up for a game of tennis, a long walk, or dining out at a cheap restaurant that catered to a guy who was always broke due to Germany's finest being prone to self-destruct.

Time passed and Jan and I grew closer. Eighteen months later she was successfully tricked into becoming my bride. The newly minted Mrs. Lambert, now being the smarter of the Lamberts, suggested that we replace the Mercedes with a car that was not constantly requiring expensive repairs. I, not being the smarter of the Lamberts, went shopping and bought a 1974 Volvo station wagon. Guess what; the Swedes design their cars for people with two left arms and a lot of extra money to give to Siegfried's cousin Sven. Everything in that Volvo seemed to be in the wrong place and that car was just as expensive to repair as the previously owned Mercedes.

These days not much has changed. Jan's current car is a very dependable 10-year-old Ford station wagon and my car is a 70-year-old Plymouth coupe. It appears that I have once again proven who is the smarter of the Lamberts.

PART TWO

NOT SO LONG AGO

Buried in the Barn

There are a lot of things that make participants in the old car hobby giddy with excitement. Near the top of the list is a "barn find" car. This is a collectible or special-interest vehicle that was tucked away in a garage, warehouse or barn and promptly forgotten. They are usually covered with a thick layer of dust or boxes filled with unused items too good to throw away, kind of like the cars that the dust and boxes are hiding from view and memory.

On a few occasions these "barn finds" have been brought to my attention and, on fewer occasions, I have purchased them and transported them to my personal barn. Here are a few examples of dusty cars that have followed me home.

The first was a very low-mileage 1954 Chevrolet 210 advertised in the classified ads of the local paper. I called and talked to the son of the car's owner, who said, "Yes, you can see the car but you must be very quiet. It's my mother's car and she's dying right now." I went to the address and  quietly knocked on the door. A middle-aged man handed me the car keys and went back into the house. From the front door I could see into a bedroom and observed several people gathered around an elderly women lying on a bed. The lights were dim and everyone was very quiet. Apparently the seller was literally on her death bed. After driving the car I quickly and quietly came to an agreement with the seller's son. I watched as he took the title to his mother and helped her with her signature. I assume that the seller expired soon after the purchase. The car itself expired about two weeks later when it let me know that, after not being driven regularly for several years, it did not appreciate being forced to travel at 70 mph for extended periods. Perhaps the seller and her car were reunited on the highway to heaven.

Barn find number two was a 1957 Buick Special. The seller had passed away seven years earlier and the car had been parked for

the duration. I made the call, paid the price, pumped up the tires, replaced the battery, changed the oil and then drove off in a car that was almost as good as new. The speedometer showed just over 30,000 miles and the car was in pristine condition. Being a Special means it was the cheapest model manufactured by Buick in 1957. It did have a manual transmission and didn't have a radio. It was barely a Buick, but I loved it and it was one of the best cars to ever have my name on the title.

Third on the list was a 1952 Chevrolet Styleline. The seller and I had a mutual friend who asked me to help the seller dispose of the car. He had owned it since 1953 and could no longer drive. I arrived at the owner's home expecting to see a rust bucket, but, instead, was greeted by an incredible example of early 1950s transportation. The odometer indicated just over 33,000 miles and the car was in excellent condition.

The seller and I talked about a price and various methods of selling the Chevrolet. "I don't want to ask too much for it but do not want to be taken advantage of either," he said. I advised him that $8,000 (this was in 1995) would be reasonable, and at this price, it would not take long to sell.

"How much would you give me for the car?" he asked. I was not shopping for another old car at that time, or so my wife and financial advisor advised me, so I told him that he would likely have an easy time selling it to someone else for $8,000. He persisted and I told him, due to limited available finances and potential second wives, that $2000 was all that I could offer. I again recommended that he put it on the market for $8,000. He thanked me for my help and we parted as friends.

The next day his wife called and said, "He'll never get around to selling it, so you can have it for $2,000." Jan, my wife, realized it really was too good of a deal to pass up and gave me her blessing to double the number of cars in the vast Lambert Automobile Collection.

Recently I discovered a real barn in Oregon that is full of dust-covered cars from the 1940s and 1950s. I wonder if Jan might enjoy a romantic Valentine's Day weekend in southeast Oregon?

Insult But No Injury

I loved my 1962 Studebaker Lark, even after it tried to kill me.

Numerous late 1940s to early 1970s collector cars have temporarily resided in my garages over the past several decades. Some were purchased because I liked them and many because they were cheap. I purchased the Lark, which was somewhere between collector and non-collector car status, in 1994. It was in excellent condition with only 30,000 miles on the odometer and had the odd charm that only Studebaker lovers appreciate.

The Lark was a very dependable daily driver during the four years I owned it. It always started and ran properly, its basic creature comforts were adequate, the heater worked and the AM radio filled the passenger compartment with music from the 50s and 60s. Everything was good with one exception; the brakes were lousy. Not just slightly inadequate; lousy, as in I might die if this damn car does not stop lousy.

I made attempts to improve the Lark's brakes with little success. The main problem was brake fade. I applied the brakes and they worked properly for a short time, but, as they heated up, they began to be less effective. The longer I applied the brakes the less they functioned, so I learned to drive a bit conservatively to compensate. This was of little help on the day of my near demise.

There is a very long and steep hill located in the city of Renton, just south of Seattle. It is about one-half mile long and anyone driving a car with poor brakes should have enough sense to avoid this hill. I guess I was a little short on sense that day.

Having knowledge of the Lark's inadequate brakes caused me to be cautious with the application of my right foot on the pedal as I began the long descent. I applied the brakes only when absolutely necessary. But the length of the hill and the degree of descent meant that the application was almost continuous. This was effective at the top of the hill and nearly negligible near the bottom.

At the bottom of the hill was a stop light that, unfortunately, was lit as bright red as Rudolf's nose as I sped towards it. The good news is that no car was stopped in front of me that I would be forced to crash into. Most of you reading this are probably thinking, "Why didn't you just jump the curb and eventually roll to a stop or, as carefully as possible, graze something that would bring you to a stop?" However, there was a steep slope to the side that would have likely turned the Lark on the road into an upside down Lark embedded in a tree. Moreover, the heavily wooded area next to the road would have provided large objects to assist the Lark's poor brakes but would likely also break me.

Instead, I decided to bring all of my driving skills into play and attempt to turn at the corner rather than drive through the red light. The car's brakes had been effective enough to slow it down to a speed that might allow for a successful right turn, but there was a possibility of starting the turn on four wheels and completing it upside down. Still, cranking the steering wheel hard to the right seemed like a better choice than running the red light.

Much to my surprise, the Studebaker successfully made the turn on at least two of its four wheels. The side street was level and led into the parking lot of a large golf driving range. The Lark rolled to a stop and I climbed out to catch my breath and regain my composure.

Could the situation have gotten any more overwhelming? Yes.

As I climbed out of the Lark I noticed a gentleman looking at me as he was loading his golf clubs into a very nice car that, I am sure, had great brakes. Much to my surprise it was my childhood friend Doug. During high school Doug and I had been very good

friends and we were two of the six founding members of the Steeds Car Club, one of Tacoma's better known hot rod clubs. In the very distant past we had ridden together many times in cars that were every bit as dangerous as my current car. I seem to recall a rather spindly 1959 MGA that Doug found to be both slow in both acceleration and stopping.

Doug, always the sensitive guy, chose his words wisely when he recognized me. There was no salutation of "Hello," or "Well, I'll be darned, it's you." No, Doug recognized me and said, "I see you are still driving a piece of #&!%."

It was great that the Lark and I were still in one piece and it was great to see Doug again.

Humpy

There is a reason that I think car people are the best people in the world.

A few years ago I had the honor of attending the Toppers Car Club's 50th anniversary party. This group of car people, many of whom I'd never personally met, made me feel like we had been friends our entire lives.

While enjoying the event I was told about a member's recent loss and the club's caring response.

Bob is a lifelong car nut and a long-time member of the Toppers. One of Bob's cars is a bit unusual--a 1938 Dodge panel truck. What makes this car even more 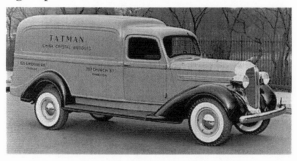 unusual is that it is a "humpback" model. The cargo area is a few inches higher than the cab, resulting in a rise or hump where the cab's roof blends into the cargo area's roof. This design feature resulted in the truck being nicknamed "Humpy" by Bob and his family.

Bob and his wife had two sons, one of whom was developmentally disabled. Son Richard's disability did not stop him from loving cars, and he especially loved "Humpy." Every day when Bob came home from work, his son Richard would yell "Humpy! Humpy! Humpy!" resulting in Bob and his son taking a short ride in the Dodge.

Another ritual was part of Richard's life; every night his mother, father and brother would sing him a lullaby when he went to bed. A complete day for Richard included a ride in "Humpy" and his bedtime lullaby.

As time went by the Dodge fell into disrepair and was left under a tarp in the garage. As Richard got older he developed an illness that eventually took his life. Something wonderful came out of this tragic event that proved the sensitivity, respect and love among car people.

Members of the Toppers Car Club and friends from the Capers Car Club decided that Richard should have one last ride in "Humpy." A dozen members worked around the clock for three days refurbishing the Dodge. The dents were removed and the body painted, the interior was reupholstered, the engine brought back to life, and all of the other details needed to give life back to "Humpy" were completed. The selfless dedication of these car people is an example of how the car community treats its own members.

During Richard's funeral service his mother, father and brother expressed their appreciation to the car people. They then stood next to Richard's casket and sang him his last lullaby.

Richard took his last ride in "Humpy" on the way to his final resting place.

Bullion Bathed Benz

Several years ago my daily driver was a very nice 1962 Studebaker Lark. Some of you may be confused by seeing the words "very nice" and "1962 Studebaker Lark" used in the same sentence. It may be even more confusing when you realize that I'm talking about a four-door sedan with a factory accessory roof rack. This is the same rack occasionally seen on station wagons and never seen on sedans. Well, almost never.

The Lark came into the Lambert corral via a local collector car auction. I had no intention of ever owning such a "grandpa car," but there it was and it was love at first sight. It was in pristine condition, previously owned by a real grandpa and, best of all, it had just over 30K original miles on the odometer. This elderwagon was very nice and was perfect for my daily travels. The auctioneer noticed that my hand was the last raised at the end of the bidding so there was no turning back. For only $3800 I now owned a very nice "Studey" or, as a friend called it, a "Stupidbaker." The purchase price was very reasonable for a car that was later featured in local and national publications and left several car shows with a trophy or two in the trunk.

One spring day I pulled up to a pump at a gas station located on Mercer Island, east of Seattle. This big hunk of dirt is famous for the waterfront homes and the residents having the highest income level in Washington State.

So there I am, pumping gas into the lowly Lark and taking in the local ambiance when in drives a totally tricked out new Mercedes Benz with everything that is removable being gold plated. Out the driver stepped and magnificent he was in his all black outfit that included a leather jacket embossed on the back with the logo of the Sonics basketball team. This guy was too short to be a player so perhaps he was just a fan, or owner, who liked embossed leather jackets and gold plating. He glanced at my Studey and looked away seemingly unimpressed. I was impressed with how he had taken his nice looking car and turned it into a brothel (I've seen them in the movies). The car did not exhibit good taste but it sure exhibited great excess. Don't get me wrong, I like cars manufactured in Stuttgart and there is one in my automotive past that was a total pleasure to drive. I'm not claiming to be the Emily Post of automobiles, but there would be a lot of gold-plated cars running around if it was considered a tasteful choice. And the golden chariot's driver may have looked upon the Studebaker as being extremely homely and he might be correct. I guess it is all in the eyes of the beholder, but this beholder was looking away from his Midasmobile.

So there sits my Lark on one side of the gas pumps and his Benz on the other. Then it happens; a few people come out of the station's convenience store and notice the cars. The grandpa car Studebaker immediately makes friends with all of them as they cast admiring glances at it and ask me a lot of questions like, "What is it?" "Is it restored?" and "What's it worth?" The low purchase price surprises them and they make congratulatory comments on what a good deal it was. Over on the other side of the pump sits the gold-covered Benz screaming out, "Hey, over here! Don't you like my gold-plated rear view mirrors, hubcaps, window frames and three-pointed hood star?" The owner's body language says he's really let down with being overshadowed by a Stupidbaker driven by a grubby guy in ripped jeans and no jacket, embossed or not.

Many readers will, perhaps, take a gold-plated luxury car over a roof-racked grandpa car any day. Personal taste is just that, an expression of what a person likes. It is likely that this bullion-bathed Benz filled the owner with pride and pleasure. Perhaps at this moment the owner may be writing a story about a homely old Studebaker with a silly looking roof rack. Yes, his automotive décor choice is just as valid as mine.

The Studebaker no longer resides in my garage. I wonder if the next owner had the roof rack gold plated?

Bigger is Better

Several years ago my family began searching for our next home. The current one at that time was just fine with one big exception, at least as far as I was concerned; it had a very small garage. The single-car garage was the original. It was built in 1927 and, like many things built in 1927, was falling apart. My wife and I, having a combined I.Q. of nearly three digits, did the sensible thing and had a new garage constructed. Good plan, right? Perhaps not. The current building codes required a thicker foundation and thicker walls. I realized too late that I had too thick of a skull to know that the new garage would end up smaller than the old garage.

We paid the contractor for his work and put the house up for sale.

Many of you know the drill; visit the open houses, talk to agents and inspect homes that are available. Sometimes homes are still available for very good reasons. "Quick access to downtown" means your driveway and the freeway on-ramp are one and the same. "Needs TLC" means the departing biker gang removed the graffiti on the walls with their fists, and "pleasant view" is of the well maintained graveyard across the street.

We spent a couple of months in the search and even made an offer on one home that we all loved. My wife and daughter made it clear that non-acceptance of our offer would somehow be considered my fault. As a result I might be sleeping in our still unsold miniature garage and my daughter might not invite me to her school's next Father/Daughter event. The offer did fail but I was eventually forgiven for not doing whatever I was supposed to do to keep the deal together. This turned out to be a good thing because very soon the perfect house did fall into our laps.

My daughter and I were dropping her friend off when the friend's parents mentioned that Edna, the nice lady next door, was considering selling her home. I placed a call and Edna invited me over. I knew immediately that the home was way out of our financial reach, but what harm would come from a quick look? Some significant things happened in the next few minutes; upon entering the home I immediately knew in what corner of the living room the future Christmas trees would be standing. This realization was accompanied by a small increase in my pulse rate. Then as we got closer to the garage the hairs on the back of my neck began to stand up. My pulse rate increased even more as Edna's tour brought me to the garage entry. The chorus of angles was about to sing.

Upon entering the garage I realized that before me was the Bat Cave, Taj Mahal (the building, not the singer) and the Playboy Mansion, or at least the Playboy carriage house, all rolled into one structure. Again I saw where the Christmas tree would be located (yes, I actually have a tree just for my garage), and visualized where my 1960 Thunderbird and 1962 Studebaker were going to be parked. They would reside in warm and spacious splendor and still leave enough room for my wife's daily driver, at least until I talked her into leaving it outdoors in the sunny Pacific NW weather so I could buy a third "but I really need this old car" car. No doubt you are dancing for joy around your living room or, more appropriately, your garage, over my good fortune. You'd better sit down because there is more.

Just off of the garage was a small room that later became known as the "car den," or, as a friend later remarked, "Lance's I love Lance Room." It was the perfect size to display decades of car guy junk while providing a place where I could feel snug and safe amongst my automotive memories and memorabilia.

I immediately contacted my family and introduced them to Edna and her home. My wife was smitten by the view (not of a graveyard but actually of a large body of water) and our daughter was thrilled that she would have her own bathroom. Edna continued giving us a tour and I again lingered in the garage and potential den. After some discussion we realized that we could come to an agreement with Edna that would result in her getting her price and us getting what had quickly become our dream home. All that would be required was that the Lamberts would have to forgo food, new clothing or participation in any form of entertainment for the duration of the 30-year mortgage.

The deal was done, we moved in and the garage was quickly filled to capacity with two old cars and too much old car stuff. I wonder if I should remodel the garage and make it just a little bit bigger?

Father Dusters

Keeping your car clean is a good thing. Keeping it too clean is, to some people, not a good thing.

My daughter and I decided to spend an evening together doing something different. Our choice was to attend an improvisational comedy group's performance at a local theater. Improvisational groups, better known as improv groups, perform skits based on suggestions from the audience. A good improv group can provide the audience with a show that will amaze and amuse. A bad improv group steals an hour or two from your life. Fortunately the evening's performers, Jet City Improv, were excellent.

Just before the intermission the group's spokesperson asked the members of the audience to go to their cars and get anything that might be a good prop for an improv scene. They would choose the best item to open the second portion of the evening's performance. My daughter and I went to my 1960 Thunderbird and retrieved a car duster from the trunk. A car duster, as many of you know, is a very large shaggy brush that has long cotton tentacles lightly coated with beeswax. It looks much more like a cherry flavored sheepdog on a stick than a brush. The brush is dragged across the surface of the car and the long waxy tentacles pick up the car's dust and leave a shiny surface. It's simple and it works very well.

So back into the theater lobby we went with the large, strange looking, bright red brush. We were standing in the lobby waiting to be let back into the theater when a woman noticed the brush and asked, "What is that?" I told her what it was and how it worked. She and her companions looked at me like I had completely lost my mind.

"You dust your car?" She paused for a moment and then asked again, "You actually dust your car?" It was at this very moment that I realized I'd tipped over into the obsessive compulsive world populated by people who count the number of steps they take and get up seven times a night to make sure the front door is locked. My daughter, a lovely young woman but also a supporter of her mother's opinion that I'm a bit compulsive when it comes to anything with four wheels, waited for my reply.

"Ah, um, yes I do. I have one in each of my cars and an extra in the garage." The woman and her companions stared at me the same way they would have if a penguin had walked into the lobby and asked to borrow twenty bucks. They couldn't believe what they were seeing and hearing.

"You see, I'm a 'car guy' and the condition of my car is very important to me. Dusting it keeps it in better condition." She, no doubt, wondered how a few billion nearly microscopic dust particles could harm a car.

She mumbled a reply and then departed to the far side of the lobby to giggle with her friends about the nut case they had just met. No doubt they looked upon my daughter with sympathy and wondered if she was beyond the age that would make calling the Child Protective Services a wise decision.

The lobby lights dimmed, we returned to our seats and, yes, you guessed it, the improv group used the car duster to open the second set of the evening. In the scene, the duster became an alien trying to take over the world.

My daughter's smile was as bright as the dust-free surface of my 1960 T-Bird.

A Final Rusting Place

    This past fall my lovely wife and I decided to take a two-week vacation that, thanks to her desire and good negotiation skills, would not include anything to do with old cars. It's not that she doesn't appreciate my love of old cars; it's just that she is exposed to it during her every waking hour that yours truly is anywhere within the reception of her ear muscles. I begrudgingly agreed and packed my already filled suitcase with a two-week supply of car magazines. You'll notice the reference to a suitcase, as in singular suitcase. My spouse, on the other hand, felt that three suitcases were needed to carry everything necessary for our trip. We would be driving a Jeep Liberty through five states famous for having temperatures in the low- to mid-seventies in October. I knew that one pair of jeans, one pair of shorts, two changes of underwear and a light jacket were all that would be needed for the trip. This choice of traveling attire was perfect, especially when I wore everything at the same time while enjoying the brisk 14 degrees and snow in the Bryce Canyon area. Her concern for my comfort was demonstrated by frequently asking, "Are you warm enough? Do you want to borrow my neck warmer? I brought three of them." I took her comments as both a loving gesture and a polite way of saying "neaner neaner neaner."

    We made it through the Great Bryce Canyon Blizzard of 2008 (actually just barely enough flakes to be qualified as snow) and headed east to admire, photograph and climb yet another giant pile of rocks the same color as the lower portion of most of the "rust free" cars that reside in our garage back home.

All was going well; the Jeep was doing its Jeepy thing, we were listening to country music and admiring the surrounding large rocks and acres of desert when (imagine a huge Chinese gong being rung at this moment) we saw "it." There before our eyes was the junkyard that every car lover dreams of discovering.

I was dumbstruck. I'm often dumbstruck, but this time I was double dumbstruck. Heck, throw a couple more dumbstrucks in there. Spread out before my wide eyes were 62 acres of rusting, weather-beaten vintage vehicles from the early 1940s to mid 1960s. We had stumbled on the Four Corners Salvage Yard in Cortez, CO.

Every automotive swap meet has at least one vendor selling prints that depict various derelict cars with grass growing through the

running boards and wheels sunk deeply into the ground. Now imagine that scene times approximately 500 cars. Do you like 1940 Fords? Take your pick. How about 1956 Chevrolets? How many would you like to take home with you today? This fender and fin final resting place even had a few hearses in residence. How is it that I had not seen this collection of dearly departed cars in any magazines, books or on a television or computer screen?

The facts were that a previous owner had gotten into an argument with the IRS that, like so many times for so many people, he lost. There was an ownership change that resulted in the junkyard now being owned by people who really did not want to own a junk yard. This explained the For Sale sign in front of the onsite garage.

I was welcomed onto the property and given a tour of the very dark and seasoned garage filled with grills, hubcaps, bumpers and various other shiny things from cars that were new when I was also new. Jim, the very helpful and friendly garage guy (hey, not every person working in a junkyard is an old crabby guy with hair growing out of his ears and a week's worth of stubble on his face), enthusiastically mentioned that everything - cars, outbuildings and the 62-acre site - could be mine for any reasonable offer. He also offered to sell just the cars. "A few months ago we were going to crush the cars for the scrap value. We had a mobile  car crusher come in to begin the job but had to cancel the plan because my phone immediately started ringing when the locals spotted the crusher. The callers let me know that I'd be the most hated man in Colorado if I destroyed a single car. How come, if these people love these cars so much, they don't buy them? They are all going to be melted down and turned into Toyotas in the near future if someone doesn't take them off my hands." His comment was a bit ironic, since sprinkled among the American automotive icons and oddballs were rusty Toyotas, Mazdas, Datsuns and even a few Teutonic vehicles, all of which must have been a bit exotic when they traversed the asphalt of Cortez.

So what was I supposed to do? Especially since I'd promised

my better half that I'd not do the car guy thing during our vacation. Among Webster's definitions for the word grovel is the word servile. I spent the remainder of the day being servile all over the place. "Yes, that vegetarian place you want to eat is the best choice. Yes, please do read aloud from your latest 'Oprah's List' book. Gee honey, you seem a bit tense. Will a neck massage make you feel better?" By the next morning she was more than happy to send me out into the 62 acres of rust and rattlesnakes with a camera in one hand and a snake whacking stick in the other hand. The next three hours were spent photographing the rusting relics and fantasizing about their former glories.

For me, this was definitely the best three hours of our vacation.

Are You the Neighborhood Crackpot?

Owning a collector car is a great hobby. But it's not a pastime for shy people. Every time you pull out of your driveway, you and the car become the center of attention. People driving by will wave, give you thumbs up, take cell phone photos and yell, "I love your car!" or "What is that?" You have the satisfaction of driving a beautiful piece of history and meeting many appreciative people. However, you will enjoy some of these people more than others. Consider these characters, for example:

THE PARKING LOT PERSON: Whenever your car has ceased forward momentum you will be cornered by someone who "had one just like it." Your car may be a restored 1957 Chevrolet convertible and his or hers may have been a four-door 1959 Ford station wagon, but as far as this person is concerned it was just like yours. It is best to listen and not argue with him or her. Also, be prepared for the question, "Did you buy it new?" Years ago I was asked that question while parking my 1952 Chevrolet. With a huge smile on my face I responded, "Yes, I was five years old in 1952 and felt that I should have my own car."

THE SLEEP INDUCER: A few admirers will want to tell you how they once rebuilt a classic car's engine / transmission / widget / whatever and then give you every detail about everything they did during the rebuild. "I think you will find this interesting: You know how the refabulation spring shaft on the transmission slurpifier is supposed to rotate clockwise? Well, this is really interesting; I took a ¾ inch beezinfliffer from a 1943 Mucklberry glove box door and turned it into a high performance counterclockwise spinning slurpifier. No wait, it gets even more interesting. First I took the….." At this point you can either hone your sleeping while standing skills, or introduce the person to any warm body nearby and then walk backwards until you are out of sight. Perhaps you think nothing is more fascinating than learning additional uses for a beezinfliffer. If so, you've just made a new best friend.

THE CHILDREN AND YOUNG ADULTS: Find me one person under the age of 18 who likes pre-1970 cars and I'll show you 1000 who do not care anything about them. Remember the old coot who lived in your neighborhood when you were a child? He was that goofy old timer who chugged down the street in the Model T Ford.

You know, the guy that you and everyone else thought was a crackpot. Well, you may now be that person. More than once I've met a neighbor who said, "Oh, you're the guy with those old cars." Not in itself a negative remark, but the tone of pity implied a lack of enthusiasm for my hobby.

THE GREENIE: These people are angry because of what they assume. These assumptions include that your car is a gas guzzling monster and that you obviously care nothing about the environment. I share with them that my 1950 Studebaker gets the same gas mileage as my 2006 Mustang. I have not tested the emissions on the Studebaker but I suspect that it is very minimal. I usually drive my collector cars less than a few hundred miles a year so my "footprint" is likely very small.

THE NORMAL PEOPLE: These people are one of the joys of the hobby. They are interested in your car and its history. They ask questions and then engage in a two-way conversation about your car and the old cars that they once owned and how they plan on getting another old car in the future. By the end of the conversation they may have told you something you didn't know about your car, and perhaps you've given them the motivation to come back into the old car hobby.

Is it worth all that it takes to be the owner of a collector car? Are you willing to put in the necessary time and expense that a vintage vehicle requires? Do you enjoy driving a car that depends on ancient engineering and 65-year-old parts to keep running? If the answer is yes, then congratulations, you've just entered one of the most interesting and rewarding hobbies on this planet.

Audible Autos

Is there a medical term for people who talk to their cars? If so, it applies to me.

I acquired my first automobile at the age of 14. My father gave me an inoperable and worn out 1949 Dodge Business Coupe in the hopes that I would gain valuable knowledge while attempting to bring the coupe back to life. The day after Dad gave me the car I asked him, "Hey, Dad, a couple of guys just offered me $50 for the Dodge. Can I sell it?" He was not pleased but gave me permission to say goodbye to the Dodge. I patted it on the fender, said adios and added the $50 to the fund used to purchase my next car--a 1948 Chevrolet Fleetline that ran great for the one week prior to the engine breaking. Yes, breaking, as in a big hole being blown out the side of the block. A friend towed the Chev home for me and we pushed it into the garage. For a few weeks I sat in the forlorn Fleetline and told it that I would soon bring it back to life. Yes, I patted the dashboard and explained that as soon as financially feasible I'd replace its broken heart with a suitable transplant and we'd be back on the road together.

Within a couple of weeks I traded a pizza for an engine that my buddy Greg had removed from his 1940 Chevrolet. Greg was upgrading to a V8, but like my Chev, I was broke and was grateful for any engine. This one was free, thanks to my employment at the local Pizza Haven.

I shared the news with the Chev, and, with substantial help from my car buddies, installed the "new" engine. The Fleetline and I were again a happy couple.

The point of these two shared memories is that I talk to my cars.

The Lambert garage protects two vehicles that I talk to almost every day--a restored 1950 Studebaker that is driven to local car shows and a 2006 Mustang convertible that is the daily driver. Due to my work schedule, it is not unusual for the Studebaker to sit in the garage for several weeks without being driven. Often, before climbing into the Mustang I'll pat the top of the Studebaker and apologize for not giving it as much attention as it deserves. These apologies are spoken out loud. An affectionate pat on the Studee's dashboard is always administered when we pull into the garage after a day on the road. I thank it for not breaking down and may even tell it when our next outing will be.

Others have told me that they also talk to their cars. We are not nutty enough to think that our cars are actually living creatures, but we are all superstitious enough to think that a few kind words here and there are appreciated by our fendered friends.

The 'Stang and 'Studee always greet me when I enter the garage. They don't actually speak words, but, instead, give me big shiny smiles when I turn on the lights. Turning on the colorful neon signs and gas pumps make them look like they are giggling with glee. The real party begins when I turn on the oldies station for music that came out of the Studee's radio speaker 50 years earlier.

Don't worry; I've never heard either car talk back to me. They are just large hunks of metal and do not come alive like the 1958 Plymouth that starred in the movie "Christine." They are, however, great listeners.

The nice lady who lives in the other parts of the house understands my odd behavior. For many decades she has seen and heard me communicating with various vintage vehicles but still allows me to hang around.

No appropriate word seems to exist for people who talk to their cars. How about "carmmunicators"?

Ballet Slippers and Magic Carpets

While recently attending my high school reunion I was struck by the large number of antique, classic, custom and hot rod cars currently owned by my former classmates. Why do so many of us care so strongly about these obsolete dinosaurs? They don't have air bags, anti-lock brakes, high fuel efficiency systems or any of the other advances of modern day cars. Yes, many have been modified with newer drive trains and safety systems, but most of them are stock or mild custom cars that mirror the cars we owned, or dreamed of owning, back in the 1960s.

In high school I knew the advantages that my lowered 1954 Oldsmobile brought me: the esteem of my classmates (at least the car crowd), the possibility of being appealing to a few more of the opposite sex (a theory believed but not proven), the ability to artistically express myself through a small amount of affordable customizing, and the perception that my masculinity was being declared by the sound of the exhaust system and the high speeds driven. These reasons, perhaps based in fantasy, were at least perceivable in my mind. But I think the real advantage, though perhaps I didn't consciously realize it at the time, was the freedom the car offered me. Freedom to escape from parental constraints, freedom to be in a cocoon with my closest friends, freedom to tell the world that I had power and that I mattered.

Academically I rated just above a turnip. In sports I could barely tell the difference between a football and a baseball. But cars I knew, and the freedom they gave I enjoyed. A cruise to Chambers Creek was always a bit exotic. Driving to Everett with my buddies to hang out with my cousin and her girlfriends always made me feel like a big shot. And

best of all was the endless cruising of Tacoma's 6th Avenue between Frisko Freeze and King's Drive-In.

It was not just feeling that we and our cars were "hot stuff."
It was the thrill of riding on magic carpets of steel and rubber,
traveling down corridors with glittering lights as we headed towards
new adventures. It was seeking out favorite places and unknown
destinations. This was the most exciting thing that had yet happened
in our lives. In our minds we were the adventurers, the pioneers, the
astronauts. And the time spent getting to wherever we ended up was
the most fun part of the adventure. Sure, what we traveled in
mattered to us, be it Bob's fast 1940 Chev, or Doug's low cruising

 1961 Olds. Even the
cruises through Point
Defiance Park in
Dave's dorky Renault
were great. It was the
feeling of freedom that
was the nectar. We
were in a ballet of
youth, discovering the
art of enjoying life. Our
cars were our ballet
slippers and the streets
were our stage.

Cars or Conversation?

Attending car shows has been my favorite activity since childhood. Every year up through my adolescence the Toppers Car Club received my $1.50 admission for their shows at the Tacoma Armory. Longtime Northwest car show promoter Clark Marshall filled the Seattle Center Coliseum in the 1960s and 1970s with attendees admiring a variety of cars, motorcycles and boats. The car show scene slowed down a bit in the '80s, but there were still occasional shows where you could stroll between the outrageous customs and classic cars. Current Seattle area shows often have hundreds of cars on display, and at least two annual shows feature up to 2000 cars. Some events are very elaborate gatherings that take a lot of planning and money to produce, while others are very casual and just provide a place to park your car for the day. Every weekend from May through October, old car hobbyists have two to ten shows to select from. By my calculations I've attended over 500 car shows since the late 1950s.

TOPPERS CAR CLUB, Inc.
Presents...
PACIFIC NORTHWEST
MOTORAMA
RODS ❖ CUSTOMS ❖ ANTIQUES ❖ BOATS ❖ BIKES
NOV. 5-6-7
TACOMA ARMORY
11th & YAKIMA
Featuring - In Person...
ED "Big Daddy" ROTH
With His Latest Car "WISHBONE"
Adults $1.50

What is it that makes a person keep going to shows that often have many of the same cars that were featured at last week's car show? Perhaps it's the love and appreciation of car design and construction. Or is it the excitement at an indoor show that includes beautiful reflecting colors, the smell of leather interiors and the familiar sound of traditional rock and roll? Outdoor shows often provide a landscape of multicolored shapes and forms that remind us of good times from long ago. Most shows also provide attendees with the opportunity to enjoy food that is not very healthy, but is very comforting. Yes, these attributes all combine to make a car show a fantastic place to spend a day. There is one other major ingredient that makes the recipe complete--being with other members of the car community. This important ingredient always satisfies the autophile's appetite.

The friendliest and most welcoming people I've ever encountered are the participants in the car hobby. Attending a car show is like attending a reunion of all of your old best friends. It makes no difference in this crowd if you are rich or poor, young or old, Republican or Democrat, religious or atheist, or of a different ethnic background. It makes no difference if you drive a worn-out four-door sedan or a totally restored convertible; you are part of the family. The most often-heard noise at a car show is not the rumble of dual exhaust pipes. It is the sound of laughter. The people laughing are often the same people that you were laughing with last weekend and will be laughing with again next weekend.

There is always excitement when someone arrives with a recently purchased beater that they have big plans to restore, or a show car that has just been completed. The driver is the center of attention as he or she climbs out of the newest addition to the car community. The proud new owner is greeted with dozens of questions: "Where did you find it? What are you going to do to it? How long did it take to build it? Is this the first time it has been displayed?" These and other questions accomplish two things; inform the fellow attendees about the car and open the door for additional communication between new and old car friends.

A few weeks ago I was sitting with a group of friends at a car show when we noticed a woman get out of a very nice 1932 Ford roadster. None of us knew her and she didn't seem to know anyone at the show. We got her attention as she walked by and we began asking her about the car. At first she was a bit awkward, but soon she was telling us all about her new toy. What she didn't know was that we were all familiar with the car because the previous owner had been bringing it to car shows for several years. The reason for our questions was not to learn about the car; it was to make her feel welcome.

The love and appreciation of old cars is the glue that holds this hobby together. Car people are passionate about their vintage vehicles and fawn over them whether they are alone or with friends, but it is better when friends are included. The most frequent problem that some car show attendees encounter is not taking enough time to look at the cars. "I have all day to look around," the person thinks, "but for now I think that I'll sit with Bill and Diane and chat for awhile." A half hour later the car owner  decides to start looking at the cars, but after walking a short distance another friend calls out, "Hey, come over here so we can get caught up." The next thing the person knows, the show is ending, the cars are leaving and several cars drive by that he or she had not noticed earlier in the day. This is an easy problem to solve; attend a car show the next weekend and take a closer look at the cars. Just be sure to leave enough time to have some laughs with a few old friends.

Dancing in the Neon

I'm going to share an embarrassing secret with you.

Many decades ago, dancing was a fun activity that I engaged in on a regular basis. My high school sweetheart and I attended all of the school dances and took great pride in dancing to every song played by the band. We even created a few routines that, we thought, assured that we were considered great dancers.

As a young man I frequented a few favorite bars that had dance floors and live music. These establishments provided single gentlemen the opportunity to ask a young woman to dance and, if a few more dances followed, possibly to begin a relationship.

I enjoyed dancing in those days but don't care much for dancing in public now. In fact, I don't enjoy it at all. The truth is that I'd rather dig ditches in my boxers during a hail storm in sub zero temperatures than dance in public. I'd rather walk down the middle of the freeway eating steamed liver while dressed as Dolly Parton than dance in public. I'd rather…well, I think you get the idea. This is why the secret that I'm about to share with you is a mystery.

I enjoy dancing in my garage.

Recently I was having a pleasant evening alone futzing in the garage. The radio was playing a rock & roll song and I was enjoying a libation. The evening was innocent and all was right with the world. My garage provides a haven where the world spins correctly and the disastrous scenarios that are unendingly yelled out of my TVs and computers are forgotten.

It was then and there that it happened.

I didn't consciously decide to begin dancing; it just happened. It was so unconscious that I was shuffling around the garage before I noticed what I was doing. Then it got even worse (better?). I really got into it. All of the old dance steps from high school came back to me and I was working up a sweat. The song ended and I stood there panting in the glow of the neon lights that grace the walls of the garage while I wondered what the heck had just happened. Was there a dangerously high level of carbon monoxide or neon gas in the garage? Were there too many paint cans with the tops left open? Had the single Corona I consumed been accidently filled with bourbon? Whatever it was, I liked it.

I was alone and didn't feel any judging eyes upon me. No one was there to correct my dance "technique" or snicker and tell me how ridiculous I looked. It was just me. Hey! Wait! That's it! The mystery has been solved; actually I was not alone. I was dancing with one of my best friends--the garage.

The garage does not judge me; it only wants to provide a sanctuary of joy and comfort. It's a place that is filled with great memories and promises of a great future. It only wants to take me by the hand and swing me around until I'm consumed with both peace and jubilance. It is my very good friend.

I've danced a few more times since then and will likely dance again. Should I be embarrassed by this activity? Are the gyrations of a slightly overweight and aging car guy dancing amongst restored gas pumps and greasy car parts to be avoided? No, because my dance partner is as happy and carefree as I am and doesn't care how silly I look.

Excuse me, garage, may I have the next dance?

Invisible Rust

Recently this car guy began actively searching for the next old car to purchase. It's time, after eight years with me, for the 1958 Rambler in my garage to occupy someone else's hallowed temple of wheels. As a result, I'm making a daily computer search in the hopes of finding the Rambler's replacement.

An online ad was advertising a 1955 Ford as, and this is a direct quote, including the all capital letters and exclamation point, "ABSOLUTLY NO RUST!" I exchanged several emails and phone calls with the seller and then left for the 160-mile roundtrip required to check out this rust-free car. Hey, nobody would be so bold as to make such a claim if it was not true, right?

Upon arriving, my suspicions were aroused when I noticed that stuck on the lower front corner of each car door was a large Ford logo sticker. When I rubbed my hand over each sticker, I could feel the bubbling rust underneath. I found another area of serious rust in the trunk lid. I brought these discoveries to the seller's attention, to which he replied, "You know, I think you're right. I've never noticed those rust spots before." This was coming from a guy who had a garage filled with car guy stuff--car show trophies, an extensive tool selection and a 1934 Ford roadster.

I expressed my disappointment and left.

My next adventure was only a 70-mile roundtrip to inspect several interesting vintage vehicles being offered by a dealer. While wandering through the cars on display, I noticed a 1964 Ford Falcon convertible. All four fenders had huge areas of rust, as did the rocker panels, resulting in this being, at best, a "drive it until it self-destructs" car, or a parts supplier for another Falcon's restoration. Any repair of the existing rust damage would cost a minimum of twice what the car would be worth when the repairs were completed. Upon returning home I went to the computer for the now-standard thrice-daily car search. I visited the Falcon dealer's web site and there were the words, "No significant rust" in the description of the Falcon. Webster's Dictionary defines significant as, in part, "full of meaning, important; momentous." Trust me, the rust was momentous.

The third sad example in this rant involves a restored 1955 Pontiac that, fortunately, was only a 30-mile roundtrip drive from home. The dealer was advertising the car as a total "bare metal" restoration that resulted in a car that "...is what it looked like on the showroom floor in 1955." I'm pretty confident that not many dealership showrooms, back in 1955, displayed new cars with rust in the driver's door and a few other places in the body. Realizing that the necessary repairs would result in too large of an investment made it an easy decision to not buy this car that the dealer had described as an "excellent example."

I went on my merry way, which included a trip back to the computer. Spotting the seller's ad on-line I, just for fun, emailed the question, "Is there any rust in the body panels of the Pontiac?" to which the seller responded "No sir, Mr. Lambert. She is clean as a whistle and showroom fresh."

So what are smart shoppers supposed to do when they find a car of interest? Ask the seller lots of questions and ask for as many pictures as you can get prior to traveling to see the car. Be very suspicious if photos of certain parts of the car are not provided. The farther away the car is located the more information you should request. Consider asking an automobile appraiser or unbiased third party in the seller's area to take a look at the car. I try to make an adventure out of my trips; I load my car up with some friends, stop for bad food along the way, check out some local sights and make it a fun day. The day I purchased my Rambler was filled with a 350-mile drive, lots of laughs with three of my car buddies and, best of all, finding a rust-free car that was actually better than described.

Good luck!

The Garage Monster

There is a frightening and sneaky monster lurking within our midst. Well, my midst anyway. Late at night this monster comes out of my midst and ends up in my garage. How do I know this for sure, since I'm usually asleep late at night? The proof is in the mess it leaves behind!

Recently I spent an entire weekend figuring out how to replace the radiator cap on my Mustang. I used every appropriate tool that I own-- a carpenter's hammer, bent screw driver, T-square from my high school drafting class and a Renault socket set that fits nothing in this part of the world. I'm sure I remembered to put everything away in its appropriate place, but that was not the case when I walked back into the garage the next morning. There were tools, bald tires, splitting boxes of old car magazines, food with hair, rags too dirty to put in the washer and beer cans everywhere. I don't even drink beer! Well, maybe just a few beers when the guys drop by or when I'm tinkering on the car or when I'm cleaning up the Mustang or anytime between 12:01 p.m. and 4:00 a.m. Every horizontal surface was piled high with a mixture of 10% good stuff and 90% useless stuff that should have gone directly into the trash or the neighbor's yard. I know that I couldn't have made this mess, so therefore, there must be a monster living in my garage.

I devised a plan that would prove the garage monster theory--video camera surveillance! Producing television's weekly "Vintage Vehicle Show" has resulted in a garage overflowing with boxes of both broken car parts and broken TV production equipment. So I set up an ancient VHS camera on an equally ancient tripod and I dropped in a long-play tape that would provide six hours of mystery-solving footage. I turned on the camera before climbing into bed and then drifted off to sleep knowing that the morning would reveal the monster at his or her or its dirty work. Not only would I solve the mystery, but I'd also have footage to sell to some crappy reality show that makes about a thousand times more money than my show does. Well, here's where the plot thickens, the mystery grows and I slip yet deeper into the grips of frustration. Not only does the videotape not show anything, but there is now junk video equipment strewn all around the garage. The dang garage monster waited until the tape ran out and then threw video junk all over the place. I know this because I'm sure that I put away everything that I didn't need in this undercover surveillance scheme.

This is a very sneaky garage monster.

The garage is now messier than ever and I have an all-weekend project coming up that will require a clutter-free area and my now-lost set of exotic tools. I need to replace the windshield wipers on Mrs. Lambert's car and I'm sure it will require all my expertise and the hammer.

I wonder if the garage monster is available to help?

Hot Pursuit

I admit it; I'm a police officer wannabe who thinks cops, and the cars they drive, are cool. This may be due, in part, to my father being a veteran of the Tacoma, WA Police Department. During my childhood he would occasionally pick me up from school, or drop me off at a friend's home, in various police cars. A few times I was allowed to push on the horn ring, causing the siren to howl on his 1950s era police cruiser. My passion for old cars, police cars included, is probably due, in part, to this early exposure. For this reason I was very excited to attend an event recently that was specifically for emergency response vehicles.

The local chapter of the Emergency Vehicle Owners & Operators Association (EVOOA) has a yearly event, held this year in Ellensburg, WA. The owners of decommissioned law enforcement

vehicles gather to kick tires, compare cars and drive them like they are in hot pursuit of bad guys. Several law enforcement agencies participate and several active and retired police officers are EVOOA members.

So what do the EVOOA members do at these gatherings?

The first night was a meet, greet and eat function where food, laughter and stories were enthusiastically shared and devoured. I felt totally accepted by the membership, perhaps due to my numerous stories of being a passenger in various police vehicles over the years, not always voluntarily. Mention of my father's tenure in blue likely also helped.

The second day started with several cars gathering at the local State Patrol office for the beginning of a caravan to a nearby police driver training facility. Included in the lineup of "Black and Whites" were a Los Angeles Police Department 1956 Chevrolet, a King County, WA Sheriff 1966 Plymouth, a California Highway Patrol 1967 Dodge, a Seattle Police Department 1968 Plymouth and a Washington State Patrol 1990 Chevrolet.

We were greeted at the driving facility, located at the Ellensburg Airport, by two Ellensburg police officers whose job it was to instruct us in the proper way to navigate the course. We first rode as passengers as they drove around the orange-coned course in contemporary Ford police cars. They had wisely decided that, despite our enthusiasm for the idea, we would not be allowed to drive these new police cars. We were, however; encouraged to take the various "antique" law enforcement vehicles through the course.

My driving began in the California Highway Patrol 1967 Dodge. The first problem was the non-power steering. This was a real arm buster that required arms more developed than mine. The second, and larger, problem was the horn ring. The danged thing was always in the way as I tried to muscle the steering wheel in one direction or another. The

owner stated that this was the way the car was originally equipped when it was a commissioned pursuit vehicle. Somewhere in the world there are a few police officers with early arthritis due to constant collisions with this ring of terror.

When I returned the car and commented on the difficulty in steering, I got an offer to drive a Washington State Patrol 1990 Chevrolet. What a giant difference! This state trooper car had no similar horn ring, was much easier to maneuver, and was also much more powerful. Some of the conditions that were hard to deal with in the old Dodge were much easier to overcome in the 23-years-newer vehicle.

An officer offered to take me along as he drove through the nearby high speed course in a new Washington State Patrol vehicle. The first time through he drove slowly as he explained what common mistakes are made during high speed driving--corners taken too wide or too tight, and frequently, too fast. Then he went through the course incorrectly to illustrate this improper driving. There was a lot of tire howling and he stated that the more howling, the more the car is trying to go sideways rather than straight ahead. Then he went through the course the correct way and maneuvered around with ease.

After the track action we were given a great presentation by a group of firefighters who fly helicopters in their efforts to extinguish forest fires. Then the caravan drove to several tourist stops, visited an impressive private collection of restored 1950s non-police cars and finished with a barbeque at one of the EVOOA member's home. Included with the burgers were lots of stories shared between the members about past police vehicle related adventures. I, of course, shared with them my newly acquired driving skills that will, no doubt, result in me being asked to become an emergency vehicle driving instructor.

I'm sitting by the phone waiting for the call.

Lowered Expectations

People who appreciate cars sometimes show their appreciation by abusing their cars. I guess I really appreciate my car.

My daily driver car is a 2006 Mustang convertible that I bought in early 2007. The "retro" Mustang design that Ford released in 2005 filled a couple of my needs: dependable transportation combined with the visual flavor of cars from the 1960s. This Mustang was for sale at a local Ford dealership and still looked showroom new despite the 16,000 miles on the odometer. The price was right and the dealership treated me fairly on the trade-in of my 1988 Saleen Mustang. After a few hours of negotiations I said goodbye to my much loved Saleen and hit the road in my "new" Mustang convertible. So far I had done no harm to the car. So far.

The first alteration I made was to replace the original homely tires and rims with Mustang GT "mag" wheels shod with low profile Pirelli tires. Low is the key word in this story. The second alteration was an excellent choice visually and a poor choice mechanically. I lowered the car. A lot.

Since childhood I've always thought cars look better lower than the manufacturers meant them to be. Lowering a car makes it look longer, leaner and meaner. I have yet to see any car that does not look better an inch or two lower than it did when it rolled out of the factory. If an inch is good, two must be better, three better yet and...

I visited the local tire store that also offered suspension alterations and ordered a set of lowering springs. Working on the premise that lower is better, I asked for springs that would drop the Mustang 3.5 inches closer to terra firma. The shop manager asked, "These springs and the weight of your car will actually make it about four inches lower. Are you sure you want it that much lower?" This may not sound like a lot but it is and I enthusiastically answered "Yes!"

Did I make a mistake?

I returned to the shop several hours later and marveled at how something as simple as lowering the Mustang made it look so much better. I happily paid the bill and cruised home. Previously I would have just "driven" home, but the car now "cruised" home due to the overwhelmingly attractive new stance. All I had to do now was convince my wife that spending $577.54 to do nothing other than lower the car was a good use of the family's funds. I'm still working on that and she still is not convinced.

Now for the explanation of the abuse previously mentioned. The Mustang now bottoms out on everything, including speed bumps, driveways, road debris, rocks, road kill and coins dropped in the street. It also rides like a tractor. We all give consideration to what will cause our final demise, and I will likely suffer from severe kidney failure due to the rough ride resulting from altering the Mustang's original and quite good suspension system.

While driving, I've developed the skill of preventing damage by spotting bumps, pot holes and debris well ahead of potential impact. I drive like I ski; I watch for problems ahead and avoid them. That system works most, but not all of the time. It may also explain why I'm a lousy skier.

Recently I was entering a gated community and did not see the large speed bump at the entry. No doubt the speed bump was placed at the gate to keep people like me out. I hit that bump at about 25 miles an hour and it sounded like a bomb had gone off under that poor Mustang. This kind of thing only happens two or three times a day.

You may ask why anyone would choose to do this to their car and their kidneys. Some wives occasionally ask their husbands that same question. The answer is easy; it looks cool and that is all the reason I need.

Big Wallets Required

Many participants in the old car hobby also collect automotive and petroleum memorabilia. The owner of a 1957 Chevrolet may also proudly display in the garage a Chevrolet dealer sign from 1957, or a restored 1950s era gas pump. Automobile dealer promotional items became useless when the next year's Chevrolets were introduced, and the Texaco gas station owner was forced to keep pace with gas pump progress when more modern pumps were designed. As time has passed, most of these items have become extremely collectible and expensive.

Recently one of the annual automotive swap meets was held at the local county fairgrounds. Hundreds of vendors were selling everything from automotive company ashtrays (great paper clip holders) to full sized automobiles. Are you looking for some factory original material to upholster your 1950 Studebaker? The vendor in stall #102 just happens to have about ten yards of it. How will a dealer's window banner announcing the arrival of the new 1940 Plymouth Road King look in your garage's window? All you need is a big garage window and a big wallet to find out--a really big wallet.

Some of the items displayed in my garage have been prized possessions since high school. A few items more recently purchased are still in the trunk of the car waiting to be unwrapped and displayed. A common thread linking these items is that they were purchased for very little money. The real high dollar items were purchased for no more than a couple of hundred dollars. OK, the old Signal gas pump cost much more, but a guy has to get himself something really special when he turns 50 years old. One of the recent additions to the collection is a plaque that was awarded to R.H. Tucker in 1950 for "...your cooperation and endeavor to develop plans toward more and better satisfied Chevrolet owners." Good job, R.H.! Your plaque is hanging next to the plaque that L.A. Sawyer received in 1951 for "Meritorious achievement in service to the petroleum industry."

"Meritorious," now that's something to fill you with pride. Perhaps things continued to go so well that future awards actually stated R and L's first names instead of just their initials. I purchased both of these plaques because they are a small part of automotive history, are great looking and, best of all, cost a grand total of $11.

Now let's return to the swap meet. I'm walking along and notice a thick paper sign approximately 11" X 17" in size advertising an auto repair shop in Tacoma, WA. It appears to be from the 1920s and features just the right amount of aging and patina to offer proof that it has been around longer than most of us have been around gathering patina. I pause, pick it up, turn it over and expect to see a price tag somewhere around $50 to $100. The price is $1500. Yes, about two or three times the new purchase price of any car being repaired in this Tacoma repair shop when the sign was clean and new. I was shocked at the price and dropped the sign as if it had just burst into flames.

I paid between $20 and $200 for many of the items in my garage. Of course the majority of items were purchased 10 to 30 years ago when a seller's pitch was often, "It's marked $20 but I'll take $15 for it." Now more often vendors say, "One of those just sold on eBay for 17 gazillion dollars but I'm willing to sell it to you for every penny you earn for the rest of your life."

These days my swap meet and antique shop sojourns are mostly for the fun of seeing a lot of interesting old car items and talking to a lot of my old car friends. I rarely purchase anything due

to the vendor's asking price and my wallet's giving price speaking different languages. Some past swap meet and antique store adventures resulted in coming home with an item that caused my family and neighbors to ask, "Why do you want that old thing?" Now the more frequent greeting is "Didn't find anything you wanted?"

Lately I've not been able to purchase some items due to the prices being too high. Fortunately that is not always the case. Last weekend I purchased a very nice old Shell "Shellmop" and container for $10. Yes, there are still a few bargains waiting for me.

Leaving the Lincoln

A good friend called a few days ago to tell me that he is selling his beautiful old Lincoln and getting out of the old car hobby. I'm still in shock.

He, like most of my close friends, has been a "car guy" for many decades. Some of us car guys (yes ladies, this includes you too) popped out of the womb with a wrench in one hand and a copy of *Rod & Custom* magazine in the other. As toddlers we played with toy cars and as we grew older we built model cars. Afternoons were spent learning to identify the make and model of the cars driving through the neighborhood. At the golden age of 16 we got our drivers licenses and soon after used money saved to buy our first cars. For me it was a 1948 Chevrolet that was purchased with the $125 earned delivering newspapers, mowing lawns and babysitting. The love of old cars is in our DNA.

Car guys spent their high school days drawing pictures of cars in class, repairing grills and other car parts in metal shop and bragging about their cars at the car guy table in the school lunchroom. At the end of the school day we headed straight for the local drive-in to show off the latest alterations to our cars and admire what our friends had recently done to their cars.

This group's love of automobiles continued to grow over the years despite life's other obligations taking on more importance. For many years, college, military, jobs, marriage and children took all of our available time and money. Some of the luckier car guys were able to still have a hot rod, custom or classic in the garage that they could work on as time and finances allowed. Many of us had to let our car passion go dormant as we trudged or sailed through our middle years. Regardless of what our circumstances were, we still had embers burning for old cars.

For many of us the passion may be based on a combination of the three Cs: creation, curves and control. We have always loved taking an automobile and creating something that we think is better than it was before we started. Most cars from the 1940s through 1960s consist of a lot of curves. My wife thinks that some of the appeal is that these cars have curves that remind us of beautiful bodies, be they a lean and muscled athlete (European sports car) or a voluptuous and Rubenesque starlet (1950s American sedan). The control aspect comes in when we buy a car, restore or alter it and then have the pleasure of driving it.

Many car guys, when asked to share their favorite moment in life, will tell you a story in which their car played a starring role. For me the story took place on a beautiful summer afternoon while driving a restored Corvair convertible on a deserted country road. The experience was the definition of bliss.

So it is with sadness that I accept my friend's decision to sell his Lincoln and leave the hobby. But it makes as much sense to me as if he had said he was no longer going to eat chocolate or play with puppies.

How is this possible? How can my friend leave his Lincoln? My car guy DNA just does not understand.

Savoring the Pits

No person in the entire world was any happier than I was on that afternoon.

There are few things that bring this car guy more joy than my family and my automobiles. My wife is going to read this so I have to list them in that order. The family segment consists of the world's greatest wife (as I mentioned my wife is going to read this) and my wonderful daughter. The automobile, on this particular day, was a fully restored 1962 Corvair Monza convertible with a Porsche red exterior, black interior, dual carburetors and an exhaust system that sounded like a tuba being played by the devil. Yes, I know, Mr. Nader said that all Corvairs were dangerous and he was right about the 1960 models, but once the suspensions were improved the Corvair became a true pleasure to drive, especially on beautiful summer days.

We owned a 44-foot 1957 Spartan Royal Mansion trailer that was located in a wooded area about 50 miles northeast of Seattle, just outside of the town of Goldbar, WA. The population in the Goldbar area consists primarily of retired lumberjacks and champion quilters. It's charming, quiet and a wonderful retreat from the "big city."

The trailer was gorgeous and looked like a diner from the 1950s. The exterior was polished, corrugated aluminum and the interior was nearly all paneled in birch with copper tile trim in the

kitchen. If Norman Rockwell had ever painted a trailer it would have looked like ours. We often spent weekends and vacations there during our 10 years of ownership, and on this particular day I was going to arrive early and the family would join me later in the evening.

While cruising in the convertible I realized that I had forgotten to bring the trailer key with me. The situation looked like this; it was a beautiful summer afternoon, the surrounding countryside was in full bloom, the red convertible was running perfectly and I had no key to get into our trailer. I wondered what to do with the several hours that would pass while I waited for my family to arrive with the key. I was hungry, so finding a meal seemed like a good way to fill some of the waiting time.

I steered the Corvair towards the nearest source of sustenance, this being the nearby town of Index. There was a general store located in Index that looked like it belonged on the main street of Mayberry, USA. The interior of the store featured worn-out wooden floors, a limited amount of the barest necessities, and every

gizmo ever invented for the fisherman. I don't fish and the trailer was already fully equipped with the barest necessities. The store also had produce so I purchased some fresh-picked cherries. I drove away from Mayberry with enough cherries to feed the entire population of Index and Goldbar.

I was now driving the much loved little red rocket

down breathtaking wooded country roads. The radio was playing hits from my high school days, there was a bag of cherries next to me and I was being warmed by the sun and the knowledge that in a few hours I would be with the two most important people in the world. True bliss was the feeling I experienced as I rapidly cruised into forest-lined curves while spitting cherry pits into the passing wind. To some readers this may not sound like the top of the pleasure list, but it was perfection to me. If you were the richest person in the world doing whatever the richest people in the world do, you were no happier than I was that afternoon.

The pits flew, the tuba blared, and I drove for a few hours while appreciating my good fortune. The cherry-stained grin on my face was nearly as wide as the Corvair. Thank goodness I forgot the key to the trailer.

Smarter Than Dirt

In the olden days, that is, more than twenty years ago, an owner of a collector car could go into any auto parts store and choose from a dozen different types of car cleaning and polishing products. Major and minor car magazines had a few advertisements for well known products that had proven themselves reliable in getting the old ride to sparkle. These days the car cleaning world has changed.

Every large car show always has a booth with a fast-talking barker spreading some miracle goop on the hood of a car. Pick up any car magazine and you will find numerous pages of car-cleaning product ads and an article or two on how to properly make your car shine "like spit on a bunny's butt." Yes, someone actually said that.

I have been washing cars for more than fifty years and I'm now going to share some of my secrets with you. Please feel free to patent, market and sell any of these secrets. You can send my royalty checks to me at your earliest convenience.

DIRT BASED POLISH: My first car was a 1949 Dodge that was dark in both color and disposition. It was sitting on blocks the day my dad gave it to me and was still on the same blocks a day later when I sold it. This neighborhood eyesore, due to a lack of tires, was unable to reach the driveway for a bath. The garden hose was too short to reach the car and this 14-year-old was too broke to buy a longer hose. For every problem there is a solution, and mine was a dirt-based product better known as dirt. Any rag or towel will work and it makes no difference if the rag is clean or dirty. Take the rag and begin shoving the dirt off the car's surface. Be sure to shake out the rag at least every half hour. What you will end up with is a car that looks clean from 50 feet away and looks like your 97-year-old grandfather's face from five feet away. People usually don't want to get any closer than 50 feet of a 1949 Dodge, so it is no big deal.

ABRASIVE-BASED CLEANER: The second car to enter this cleaning research scientist's life was a 1948 Chevrolet. It had been repainted bright yellow and the exterior appeal was improved by spraying a couple of areas with gray primer. Trust me; this was a cool thing to do in 1963.

How did I keep this now age-spotted chariot clean, you ask? Easy, I scrubbed it with Comet. Yes, the same product that you use to get your pots, pans and children really clean. The application consisted of spraying water on the car, shaking on some Comet and scrubbing with a sponge. Believe me, the car ended up really clean. The driveway looked great too with its new layer of paint particles that, just a few moments ago, were securely attached to the car. Current hot rod and custom car owners are applying what is referred to as suede paint, a paint that appears dull. I guess the car hobby can thank me for being a pioneer in getting rid of that distracting shiny surface on cars.

ONE-STEP CLEANER and POLISH: Car number three was a very nice 1954 Oldsmobile that was lowered three inches, shod in reversed wheels and sounded like a yodeling Darth Vader. I had matured to being a wise 17-year-old who knew that cars needed cleaning products that cost a lot of money, or at least more than a can of Comet. The latest rage was a product that claimed you did not need to wash your car before applying: it would wash and wax your car at the same time. What the product did not mention was its ability to wash the paint, wax the paint and remove the paint all in one application. The surface of the merry Oldsmobile always looked great until one day I noticed that the underlying primer coat was looking back at me. The cleaner worked so well that it cleaned and waxed my paint until it was gone. Oh well, soon I was moving to an exotic foreign country (Hawaii) and I needed to sell the car anyway.

SINK SOLUTION: The next few dozen cars were washed with anything that would create bubbles and a false sense of getting the job done. I'd grab whatever dishwashing detergent that was under the kitchen or bathroom sink, or shampoo from the shower and add it liberally to a five gallon bucket. The addition of water resulted in lots of bubbles so it must be an excellent way to get a car clean. This method worked so well that it took off all of the dirt and also any coating of wax. The lack of wax eventually took a toll on the paint but it didn't matter because the cars looked great for at least an hour after they were given a "lemon fresh" or "dandruff free" scrubbing.

CURRENT CLEANING ADVICE: My final cleaning and polishing tip is to hire a professional to detail your car, then park it in the garage under a car cover and keep it clean by never driving it. Then drive your spouse's eight-year-old station wagon and keep it sparkling by occasionally running it through the automatic car wash at the gas station.

Car Friends

As I sit at my desk looking out the window, the realization is sinking in that the car show season is over. No more wandering through parks or parking lots full of classics, customs and hot rods. No more unconsciously singing or whistling softly because I'm in an environment that makes me very happy. No more not being able to walk 50 feet without running into a car friend. Sure, over the winter there is always a car club meeting or party to attend, or a car buddy to visit and help with a project. But these activities don't compare to parking amongst acres of carnival colored cars and being surrounded by equally happy car friends.

Our common love of cars is a strong bond. I don't care who you voted for in the last election or what numbers are on your W2 form. I don't care that I'm old enough to be your father or young enough to be your son. What I care about is that you and I talk the same language and share the same passion. Your passion may be for 1960s cars with blowers sticking through the hoods, or for 100 year old contraptions with shiny brass trim gleaming in the sun and steam chug chugging out of the tailpipes. You may make some choices with your car that would be different choices than I would make. But regardless of our preferences we understand each other's passion for cars. You accept me for or despite these differences because you are a car friend.

You are the one that encourages me to wake up at 5:30am on a weekend so we won't be late to a car show or cruise. You appreciate the rolling sculptures that surround us on the grass or asphalt as much as I do. You are full of life, quick to laugh, always supportive and eager to share your knowledge and labor. You reflect the best parts of life. You are why car shows are so much fun. The cars on display are great but your friendship is greater. The cars are the cake and you are the frosting. My world is not so narrow that it only allows me to have friends in the car hobby, but these friends are a top priority.

Now I'm going to have to go through the winter without hanging out at a car show with you. It's going to be a long winter, but of course I'll get through it. There are things that need to be done on the car and the garage always needs to be cleaned up. But for the next several months I'll miss seeing you at shows and having you excitedly point out the latest improvements to your car. I'll miss our laughing together as we recall some past car show incident. I'll miss walking by the cars and telling you what I like about certain ones.

Stay warm in your garage this winter. I'll see you at the first spring cruise or show & shine.

Confessions of a "Joiner"

Unfortunately I have many bad habits: eating junk food just before going to bed, procrastinating on everything, getting irritated when other drivers don't drive as well as I do and, worst of all, joining car clubs.

Since high school I have been a member of at least 20 car clubs, with a level of commitment ranging from never attending meetings, to being a founding member and four-term president. These clubs ranged from rowdy gatherings of car nuts to meetings run like a military drill team. Most car clubs have the same thing in common; they are proud of their club and their cars. Every club provides the opportunity for various levels of participation, from active leadership roles to occasional attendance at club functions. A club's personality is usually a reflection of the cars. Hot rod and custom clubs are very casual and fun loving, clubs with high value classic cars are well organized and active, and sport compact clubs place as much value on the sound systems as the motors. I've belonged to clubs that had no dues, and one club that cost more than $1200 per year for membership. With this background, I'd like to make a recommendation to you; join a club. It will provide you with additional sources for parts and advice, expose you to likeminded people, give you many choices of events and social gatherings to attend. Best of all, it will help you maintain enthusiasm for your car.

Helping to start the Steeds Car Club in 1962 was a wonderful early experience in organization and in building self-confidence. The following five decades included membership in many clubs. The Ford Owners Association provided 11 years of going on road trips together, attending parties at each other's homes, and helping to raise money for charitable causes. Four years in the Heartland Vintage Thunderbird Club provided hands-on training in T-Bird repair.

Membership in Mustangs Northwest meant gaining additional knowledge and appreciation of Mustangs. The Steeds, dormant for a few decades, have re-formed and recently celebrated the club's fiftieth anniversary. I've had the pleasure of being the newsletter editor, events coordinator and president for the past four years.

Is there a dark side to belonging to a club? Read on.

There was the go-kart incident when the Ford Owners Association held its yearly go-kart race. The night before the race my fellow members made arrangements with the track owner to alter my kart to assure a last-place finish. That plan worked until I decided to intentionally drive across the grass infield to re-emerge in first place. The track owner aggressively suggested my early retirement from racing for the day. The other racers finished out the day by barricading my motel room door with patio furniture, resulting in my not being able to open the door. The Rusty Relics asked me to step down from my long-held car show emcee position due to some attendees not appreciating me demonstrating my sterling sense of humor onstage. The Rat Pack Car Club's weekend drive resulted in a bent piston rod as my six-cylinder 1952 Chevrolet tried to keep up with the rest of the V8 pack. A Corvette Marquee Club event resulted in me drinking a bee that had landed in my margarita and, at that point, I no longer cared. An Avanti Owners Association event resulted in a woman going out of her way to walk up and say, "I can sure see why they stopped making these. You own the ugliest car that I've ever seen".

If you join a club, the worst thing that can happen is you will be out a small amount of money. The best thing is you will be provided the opportunity to enjoy every aspect of owning a special-interest car. This enjoyment includes making new friends and having opportunities to work with various charities sponsored by the clubs.

A Gentleman's Ride

Yesterday started with me getting upset over a few very trivial things. The day ended with a deeper appreciation of what is truly important in life.

Here's how it happened: A collector car owner called and made an appointment to have his car appraised. He owns a beautiful 1956 Oldsmobile 98 convertible and wanted to establish the market value. On the phone he did not mention the reason for the appraisal, and I was too frazzled to ask.

That's because the day of the appraisal appointment started with me spilling coffee beans on the floor and then stepping on one. It broke and I had to walk 10 feet to get a broom and dustpan and then walk the 10 feet back to clean up the tiny mess. I utilized a few four-letter words as I swept the aromatic remains into the dustpan. "I don't have time today to deal with this inconvenience," I announced to the world. "Inconvenience" was not the actual word I spoke.

A short time later I was sitting at my desk attempting to open a program on the computer. It was taking too long, and I grumbled a few more profanities. Damn! Was the whole day going to be this frustrating?

A few hours later I left for my appointment to inspect the gentleman's car. I was running a little late and realized that I'd misread the map and was well past my destination. What a frustrating day! A call to the client got me correctly oriented and I arrived about 15 minutes late. Pulling into the driveway I noticed the client waiting as he steadied himself with his walker. We shook hands and he began sharing information about his award-winning car. It was then that he asked, "Do you want to drive it?" I stated that usually I didn't drive clients' cars for fear of doing some damage to the vehicle or having it self-destruct with me behind the wheel. But he insisted that I drive the car, so we climbed in and drove down the wooded two-lane road leading away from his home. As we rode, his motivation became apparent.

He had not driven or ridden in the car for more than two years and his health was so poor that he could not even wash the car, although it still radiated flash and class through the layers of dust.

"Can we just drive for a while?" he asked. "I can no longer drive and I'd just like to enjoy my car again." It became obvious that

150

this was likely one of the last rides he would ever take in his beloved car.

"Of course we can. Where shall we go?" I replied. We drove along many miles of wooded roads as he shared with me the history of the car and his love of the old car hobby.

"I used to attend car shows but have not been to one in a few years," he told me. "I'm blind in one eye and losing my sight in the other. The nerve endings in my hands are going and I have trouble feeling anything that I touch. I also have Parkinson's." At that moment I thought about my frustrating morning dealing with one crushed coffee bean and a slow computer. I felt a bit foolish.

This gentleman was going to be my co-pilot and navigator for as long as he wanted the drive to last.

The car ran perfectly despite not being driven for a long period. "The gas in the tank is two years old so it may not run properly," he said. However, it ran like it had been tuned up the day before. We drove through wooded areas, past open fields and into small rural communities as he shared adventures that he'd enjoyed in this car.

He asked if I would stop at a gas station and put a few gallons of fresh gas in the tank. As the tank was filling, the station attendant walked up and began admiring the beautiful Oldsmobile. I motioned to the owner sitting in the car and he began telling the attendant about the stunning red and white convertible. During the brief conversation he sounded very happy and very healthy.

The time too quickly passed and we returned to his home. The car sat majestically in the driveway as I continued with the inspection and he shared more of the car's history. When he wasn't talking he just sat staring at the car and smiling. I will never forget the smile on his face.

After about an hour I completed my inspection, thanked him and departed.

The sun was peeking through the clouds so I put the top down on my Mustang convertible to better enjoy the drive home. While driving I thought about how my day had started and the experience with the gentleman and his car. He was dealing with the loss of his health and his car while I was enjoying the sun in the sky and the wind in my hair.

Nothing else upset me during the rest of that day.

Perfect Parking

My wife, a truly lovely woman, and our daughter, the pride of my life, keep picking on me. They think they are giving me good advice, but, to the contrary, they are totally wrong about the topic: parking.

Parking is something about which I am a true expert. At the age of 18 I actually made a portion of my living as a valet at a posh restaurant frequented by posh people in posh cars. You can always tell a restaurant is posh when the parking staff are called valets rather than parking lot attendants. The patrons trusted me to park their symbols of success and, therefore, this qualifies me as an expert valet. It is very similar to getting a Ph.D. or honorary degree in the field of parking. Unfortunately, Mrs. and Miss Lambert fail to recognize my expertise.

Here's the usual scenario: we are out for dinner, shopping, whatever, and pull into a parking lot. Instantly my parking lot survival skills come into play. Which spot is the least likely to result in getting any door dings or scratches? What spot assures that any vigorous door opening into another car by a Lambert will not result in a punch in my nose, a visit to small-claims court or both? More importantly, which small piece of paved real estate "talks" to me? Yes, I have developed the amazing knack of communicating with asphalt and concrete. As I cruise through the lot I listen for the whisper of, "Hey, over here. This is a perfect spot." It always comes. It's surprising that it can be heard above the female passenger's unending "Where are you going? What's wrong with that spot? Daaaaad, are we ever going to park?" It may take five to ten minutes of trolling to find the right spot, but it always materializes. One spot may be too small by four inches. Another spot is not acceptable because it is where a runaway shopping cart might take aim at our family chariot. Shopping carts will actually travel uphill just to damage our car. We continue our search, but the next open spot (the one that is being pointed out with shouts of, "Take that one! Why don't you take that one?") is just not right. I'm kind of like Goldilocks trying out various bowls of porridge.

What, you ask, is the "perfect spot"? There must not be any cars next to the spot. It can't be within any measurable distance to the shopping cart drop-off corral. It must be visible from inside the destination. It can't be too close to the parking lot entry or exit. It can't be under anything that will support birds of any type. Any curb next to it cannot be higher than three inches. It can't be directly next to any building, display, storage facility, charity drop-off container, dumpster or piles of anything. I must "feel good" about any nearby cars and they must be less than three years old and have an original purchase price of at least $50,000. The parking spot can't be where any road debris is or might be. It must be clean and puddle free. The spot must provide a clear visual field when I back out. I think you will agree that these are all understandable requirements. Anyone not agreeing is either an unskilled car parker or a Lambert other than me.

All of these requirements are totally reasonable; however, my wife and daughter have yet to recognize this and my amazing ability for locating just the right parking spot. Yes, perhaps it is a quarter mile from our destination or a thousand feet from any nearby car but the ladies usually end up reluctantly agreeing that, indeed, it is a great parking spot. The time it takes for us to walk from the car to the destination provides ample time to discuss my successful parking strategy, or at least point it out to my passengers.

I am, after all, a valet.

Roth's Wrath

Anyone who has an appreciation for the old car hobby knows the name Ed Roth. Ed "Big Daddy" Roth was a prolific artist, custom car and motorcycle builder, model car designer and automotive entrepreneur. Bid Daddy definitely was and remains an icon in the old car hobby. Ed passed away in 2001 but he left behind one enormously enduring icon: Rat Fink.

Rat Fink is a large, very unkempt rat that Ed drew on shirts that he sold at car shows and by mail order, starting in the late 1950s. Rat Fink always has flies flittering around his head and drops of sweat flying off his torso. Having a Rat Fink shirt was a big deal back then, and thousands of Rat Fink shirts are still sold every year.

When I was 12 years old I had just enough artistic talent to do a rendering of the Rat Fink that was recognizable. It by no means was anywhere close to the great drawing quality that Ed was capable of, but it was close enough to provide my 12-year-old hands with a way to create a little bit of spending money.

The kids in my neighborhood would bring me their T-shirts and sweatshirts and I would use a marking pen to draw Rat Fink on the backs of the shirts. Mr. Fink always had his eyes bulging out, his sharp and crooked teeth gleaming and several flies buzzing around his head. I'd draw the rat and then spray it with yellow, orange and green fluorescent spray paint. The fee for my efforts was 50 cents and, at the time, this was a significant amount of money for a 12-year-old to have in his pocket.

I continued this flagrant plagiarism until many kids in the neighborhood were adorned in Rat Fink attire. The demand for the shirts then declined, so I changed careers and did what every young boy in my neighborhood did to make money--I got a paper route. It was the end of my Rat Fink rendering career but not the end of my Ed Roth admiration.

Decades passed, and then in August of 1993 my brother Jay and I were in Reno, NV attending "Hot August Nights." This is one of the largest hot rod and custom car events in the world and usually has about 5000 cars attending. It's approximately a week long and includes everything imaginable related to the old car hobby: famous custom car builders, famous custom cars from the '50s and '60s and current creations that emulate the traditional custom styles. This particular year included a personal appearance by Big Daddy himself. Ed always drew a large crowd of fans and I became just another person seeking a little of his time.

I had no idea that he was going to threaten me.

I saw Ed talking to some fans so I walked up, hovered nearby and finally introduced myself. To illustrate my admiration and respect for his talents I decided to share the story of my past efforts to copy his style on the neighborhood kids' shirts. I didn't expect the reaction that resulted.

Ed was a very large man and, not unlike the Rat Fink, tended to tower above the people around him. Upon hearing my story he put his hand on my shoulder, bent over and nearly touched my nose with his as he uttered, "Well, son, then I guess you owe me some money." He paused just long enough for me to begin sweating like Rat Fink, and then he began laughing. I joined in the laughter and, because I wanted some of his artwork and felt I did owe him some money, purchased a drawing of another of his cartoon characters and asked him to autograph it.

Ed has been gone for a decade but you'd never know it. His talents continue to appear in various automotive and graphic design publications, his cars are still featured in car shows and museums and, perhaps best of all, you can still purchase a T-shirt with the grimy and crusty old Rat Fink on it. Ed, like Elvis, is still very successful even after his demise.

Diamonds in the Dealership

The collector car hobby is not just about old cars. Within the hobby are people who love old signs as much as old cars.

At one time all old cars were new cars sitting in, or ordered from, a new car dealership. The dealership was surrounded by signs identifying the manufacturer and also signs boasting about the incredible attributes of these cars. Some featured "Jetaway" and "Torqueflite" transmissions, "Jetfire Rocket" and "Blue Flame" engines and "Vista-Cruiser" and "Hornet" styling. The late 1940s through late 1960s were the best years for bombastic verbiage and hyperbole. To many car collectors, the signs and showroom displays from that era are just as exciting as the cars.

Service station signs are also highly sought after by collectors. A large Texaco or Shell sign always makes a car lover's garage or family room more festive. Signs proclaiming the virtues of "No-Nox" or "Fire Chief" gasoline usually bring a smile.

This has not always been the case. For years these advertising accessories were displayed and then abandoned when the new model year's promotional items arrived or the next ad campaign began. The preceding model year's items or gas additive proclamations instantly became junk and soon were added to the local landfill. Fortunately, many items were banished to the dealer's storeroom or attic. As time went by these items became desirable to car buffs, and some lucky old car aficionados were able to get their hands on them. Most of the time dealers thought the signs and displays were just junk taking up space and were glad to get rid of them. "You want that piece of junk? Sure, you can have it. Get it out of here." The happy recipient was thrilled to have a flashy sign to hang in the bedroom or garage. What is more attractive than a huge "Wouldn't You Rather Have a Buick?" or "See the USA in a Chevrolet" sign hanging on a car collector's wall? If a sign included neon lighting, then you had the most desirable sign of all.

I began collecting signs in the 1960s. Two signs in the collection were actually retrieved from dumpsters. Unfortunately, times changed and dealers realized they had items that people were willing to purchase. What was free began selling for $10 or $20, and a few decades later these same signs began selling for $200 to $20,000 each. Yes, there were four zeros in that last number. I'll warn you now that you should sit down before you finish reading this article. A friend of mine just paid...well, I'll get to that in a moment.

Many of us could not afford to buy today the signs we obtained in the past. The $20 purchase made in 1985 may now be worth $2000, but most of us don't care about the monetary value. It's about how fantastic they look hanging in the garage, not about how much they are worth.

For the past 20 years my hosting of television's "Vintage Vehicle Show" has taken me many places and I've been fortunate to see incredible collections of signs. A few of these collections are owned by some of the most famous icons and celebrities in the automotive and entertainment business. But most are owned by the average person who spent his or her hard earned dollars to occasionally purchase an additional sign to hang in the garage.

There are still good deals available for the dedicated collector who is willing to search hard for a bargain. Recently I purchased a large 1920s sign advertising automotive electrical parts. It felt like 1975 again when I handed over a whopping $18 for the sign. At the other end of the spectrum is a sign recently purchased by a friend. He began collecting signs 12 years ago and now has, perhaps, the best collection in the world. He recently paid $44,000 for a sign advertising a brand of oil from the 1940s. This 2' X 3' piece of metal is more valuable than many items displayed in a jewelry store.

I warned you to be sitting down before you finished reading this article.

Floating, Flying and Fraternizing

OK, here's the question: you take four aging car guys, add a funky houseboat, an ancient airplane, a super sports car and what happens? I found out a few weeks ago when I spent five days with three of my best high school buddies.

Hector (not his real name) lives in a houseboat in Portland on the Columbia River and has a 1979 Grumman Tiger airplane to entertain his pals. Gunter (not his real name) flew in from Washington, D.C., to join in the melee and Obadiah (not his real name) extracted himself from the social cave he'd been hiding in for 40 years to spend some quality time with his less-than-quality friends from the olden days. It was going to be the perfect mini vacation and we were equipped with all the essential tools--floating accommodations, winged transportation, impressive sports car and beer. Perfect!

Gunter arrived at my Seattle doorstep and we sped off in a borrowed 2007 Mitsubishi Eclipse GT Spyder utilized for our Speed Racer bonsai run to Oregon's Land of Ports. The best description of this classy four-wheeled rocket is, well, it's really classy and goes like a rocket. The combination of Japanese engineering and an overconfident belief in my driving ability provided Gunter with a reason to consider a return trip on Amtrak.

Rapidly we headed south, and in no time we were sliding sideways into Hector's driveway. We unloaded the essential cargo (beer) and made our way onto the USS Budweiser. Obadiah soon arrived and we all settled in to sitting, sipping and reminiscing about our days of high school sub-par scholastic accomplishments and automotive near-death experiences.

Gunter, known since high school as "Crazy" (not his real nickname), once again shared the story of partially removing the roof from his 1948 Chevrolet four-door sedan and loading the "convertible" with 8 of his buddies. He then commenced careening around the neighborhood as the Chevy's altered roofline caused it to look and handle like a giant, half-opened sardine can.

Hector reminded us that his proud accomplishment was having puked out of the window of nearly every one of his high school buddies' cars, an honor only surpassed by his reputation of being able to destroy the rear tires of his 1963 Plymouth Fury on a weekly basis. And Obadiah, long respected for his ability to not get beat up by his hot rod cronies for driving a 1959 VW, once again shared his expertise on where in the VW's engine compartment to keep the pizza warm and where in the trunk to keep the beer cold.

I (not my real name) once again spun and embellished the tale of how my high school sweetheart would remind me that no, my 1954 Oldsmobile was not the reason that she tolerated me and, in fact, she still dated me despite the car. That dear old Olds was known affectionately as "The Boat Anchor" by Hector, Gunter and

Obadiah.

The sojourn included a laughter and terror filled flight in the 27-year-old airplane, a few beer bottles sent floating down the Mighty Columbia, and fond farewells shouted as the Japanese dream machine headed back to the home of the Space Needle.

It sounds to me like we created five brand new "good old days" of adventure.

Garage Guys

Jan and I purchased our home 20 years ago. She bought the view and I bought the garage. We both got the house thrown in with the deal. The garage, fortunately, is located close to some other car guys' garages.

The closest in location is Rick, the proud owner of a 1984 Jaguar convertible. Rick owns a very rare car--a dependable Jaguar. The cost of Jaguar ownership recalls a line Woody Allen spoke when he was playing the role of a stock broker in a movie: "I invest people's money until they don't have any left." Rick's convertible seems to be the exception to the rule, and the Lambert Automotive Museum will be very happy to relieve him of ownership anytime. Thus my constant question, "How's it running?" that tactfully hides the subliminal message that his Jaguar will likely self destruct at any moment and, therefore, he should sell it to me for a very cheap price.

Just up the street is Jim, whose collection includes a 1949 Mercury, a 1957 T-Bird and a plethora (no, it's not the name of a car) of mysterious vehicles that show up one day and then vanish like the morning mist. Jim is the kind of car collector who says, "Oh that (fill in the blank), it's just something that I've had forever." The "just something" is usually a car for which I'd be willing to hand over my grandmother to pirates.

To the south is Joe, who is using his computer building skills to construct a reproduction Shelby Cobra. Some of the locals and I stop by his garage on occasion to lend a helping hand in putting

together what seems like a really big model car kit. Joe usually spends the following day repairing any damage that is the result of my "help." He has a big dog residing in the garage that always barks

at me. The barking is usually the most intense when Joe says, at the same time that he's filling my pocket with a live squirrel, "Don't worry, the dog doesn't bite." Obviously Joe loves to have me stop by for a visit.

Heading north finds the tour in front of John's house, which is usually surrounded with a bevy (again not a type of car) of hot rods. Someday, when I grow up, I want to be just like John. He, unlike this neighbor to the south, knows which end of a screwdriver to hold, and that there are tools other than a hammer to use for the majority of auto repairs. John drives the finest 1936 Ford roadster in the galaxy and usually the entire neighborhood can hear him driving down the street. My response is charging out of our house like an eight-year-old kid when he hears the Good Humor ice cream truck coming down the street.

There have been a couple of car guys who have left the area in the past few years. I'd like to think that they were just moving on with their lives and that the move was not the result of my constant dropping by to visit and ask, "What are you doing? Are you going to work on your car today? Can I help?"

One of these vacating (fleeing?) neighbors was Jerry, the king of all things Thunderbird. He owned two T-Birds, a 1957 and a 1966 that were sterling examples of how cool these cars are. You would often see these vintage vehicles at various local parades and car shows with the chrome shining as bright as the smile on Jerry's face. He probably moved because his garage was no longer big enough to hold all of his car show trophies. Or perhaps he was tired of cleaning off this snoopy neighbor's nose prints from his garage door windows.

Bob, another former neighbor, was more my kind of car guy. He recognized that the world was full of very desirable cars that can be purchased for next to nothing. My dad once traded one of his cars for a box of chocolates and a bowling ball, but that's a story for another time. Bob's "bowling ball" cars were often the lesser models manufactured by the Chrysler Corporation. Bob would take a bland and plain model, add new paint and upholstery, rebuild the engine, and end up with a car that, like my college girlfriend Sonja, was really beautiful once you took a closer look.

So what's the point of this tour bus through your scribe's neighborhood? Seek and ye shall find? Fences, and locked garages, make good neighbors? Every village has an idiot? I think it's a warm and fuzzy story about how a person can enjoy the company of like-minded people located on the home turf. I just hope that they don't sic their dogs on you or flee the neighborhood in search of some privacy.

Look But Don't Touch

There are two types of people who participate in car shows-- the car owners and the general public attending the show. The majority of the first type, the owners, are either a little crazy or totally off their rockers. The second type, the public, is made up mostly of healthy people with a few nut cases sprinkled in.

Most people who display their cars are reasonable human beings who lead productive lives, are kind to animals and will give you the shirt or blouse off their backs. That is, until you touch their car at a car show. For some reason these cars that have been around for many decades will instantly turn to dust if they are touched by anyone other than the owners. I've seen owners almost end up in fights when someone touches their candy-apple-painted baby. I should know, because I'm one of them.

Over an eight-year period I displayed my restored 1960 Thunderbird at about two hundred car shows. I once had a father and son walk up and open the hood, which is not easy because you have to pull a lever under the dash to pop it open. Their defense was that they were restoring a 1960 T-Bird and wanted to see the engine compartment. At another show I looked over to see a young lady sitting in my car pushing the radio buttons as fast as she could. I walked over and, as calmly as I could, told her that the appropriate

etiquette at a car show is to look and not touch, and you certainly don't climb into the car and hammer away at the radio. As she got out of the car, something on her bib overalls caught a portion of the upholstery and ripped out a button from the seat cushion. I'm a gentle man who will generally seek out the most non-confrontational way to solve problems. Not this time! I went nuts as I screamed at her for the damage she had done to my car. She responded by looking at me and saying casually, "Jeez man, chill out." I had two choices: remove her head or walk away. I quickly contemplated spending the rest of my life in prison and decided that walking away was the best option. Saint Peter should give me an extra cloud in heaven for that act of composure.

So what's my point? It's like she walked up to a stranger's house and entered without knocking first and being invited to enter.

Ask car owners about their cars and you may even be invited to sit in the car. You'll definitely have any questions answered by the car's proud mama or papa. A few car owners will even let curious children sit behind the wheel and honk the horn. That is, unless they are wearing bib overalls.

Nerd Cars

Recently, while attending a monthly car club meeting, I heard the words that I get an odd pleasure hearing.

"I hate those cars!"

Another club member asked if that was my Studebaker in the parking lot. I said yes and he asked why I would want to own such a "nerd" car. My Studee is not just a Studebaker; it's the nerdiest of Studebakers. It is a 1962 Lark four-door sedan with a factory installed luggage rack on the top! He said he hated it and all Studebakers, Ramblers, Corvairs and a few other cars that have a history of being considered undesirable by a segment of the old car hobby.

Prior to purchasing the Lark I was in Portland at an auction where I ran into a fellow member of a Ford-based club. He asked me what I was looking for and I told him a Studebaker. He responded with "Studebaker! You don't spell that F-O-R-D!" He then turned his back on me and walked away.

It's people like these who make owning nerd cars oddly appealing.

When I purchased the Lark at a different auction it had traveled just 30,000 miles and was in excellent condition. A well known automobile collector publication covering the auction singled out the car and described it as being in "excellent near perfect condition." I couldn't believe it when I first saw the car. It looked like a new car sitting on the showroom floor. The original owner, now in his 80s, had taken exceptional care of the car. You know the story (only to church, shopping, etc). The Studebaker is now my daily driver and I'm constantly getting thumbs up and favorable comments. It took first place in its class at a past Studebaker International Convention and has taken a first place and second place at two Studebaker Can-Am Meets. Its most recent competition in concours judging gave it 388 out of a possible 400 points, and that was with losing four points for not having stock radiator hoses.

What's my point, you ask? I paid $4200 (including tax, licensing and auction commission) for the car. That's a lot of value for such a small investment.

The Studebaker is not the only nerd car that I've purchased. I recently owned a beautiful 1962 Corvair Monza convertible. It had a five-year-old complete restoration when I bought it. It was red, fast and loud and it received constant attention, mostly positive. Mostly, but not always. A woman walking by it at Super Chevy Sunday a few years ago commented to her companion, "What a cute car." He grabbed her arm, and while pulling her away, said, "It's just a f*****g Corvair!" A guy walked by at a car show and asked me, "Why don't you buy a real car?" I find this attitude both irritating and satisfying. Irritating because the car is not appreciated and satisfying because this attitude keeps cars like Corvairs extremely undervalued. This red convertible cost me $4500 and that is mighty cheap for a convertible in great condition. The people who denigrated the car were definitely in the minority. At show & shines I would leave a copy of Ralph Nader's "Unsafe at Any Speed" on the dashboard. It always got a laugh when people noticed the book. Nader was wrong, but thanks in

part to him, Corvairs are a great car for little money. I've owned dozens of 1940s to 1960s cars, both nerd and cool, and this one was one of the most fun to drive.

I've owned several Ramblers and I'm considering buying another. It's a 1958 Rambler that took best of show at the 1991 Rambler National Convention. I was there and watched people go nuts over the car. It's in breathtakingly gorgeous condition as the result of a total restoration. This car is a great example of "warm and fuzzy." It has been driven approximately 500 miles since 1991 and the owner wants only $4000 for it. That barely covers the cost of some repair work on a more "desirable" car.

I understand investing in more desirable cars. Cars that make your heart pound in fear if you see anyone within five feet of them. Cars that are so valuable that they are only driven on sunny days when the temperature is over 75 degrees. I own a fully restored bright red 1960 T-Bird with wire wheels. It's my first choice for displaying at car shows. But the Studebaker allows me to drive a great car every day. It is a car that I can enjoy and not be overly concerned if it wears out or is destroyed (nerd cars are rarely stolen).

Owning a nerd car provides you with an inexpensive opportunity to drive a collector car and participate in car club activities and car shows. You can even park it right next to the cool and desirable car that is being guarded by the nervous owner.

EPILOGUE: An addition has been made to the Garage d'Lambert since this article was written. The latest arrival is considered by some people to be the nerdiest car ever manufactured; a 1950 Studebaker Champion four door sedan. I've always loved "Bulletnose" Studebakers and it's a dream come true for me to own this restored beauty.

What's That Noise?

You are about to learn why wives should not be allowed to ride in their husband's hot rods, customs, special interest or any other kind of "old car." There's a reason for this bold and perhaps foolish statement. Foolish in that it may provide my wife with the initiative to pour tonight's dinner on my head.

Old cars, like old car owners, have a few recurring creaks, thumps, rattles, exhaust leaks and other audible messages that let the owner know that time is marching on. But many old car owners, me included, barely notice. And neither do my guy friends. Guys, as in husband-type guys. Whenever they join me in a vintage vehicle adventure, we just travel merrily along with the rock and roll blaring and the mufflers barely muffling. I notice nothing other than the tunes coming out of the dash and the rumbling coming out of the rear end (the car's, not mine). All is well. Not so when the lovely Mrs. Lambert climbs aboard.

"What's that rattling noise?" "Does the car always make that funny sound when you accelerate?" "Why does it smell so much like gas in here?" (again the car, not me). "How come the glove box door keeps falling open?" "How come the heater won't turn off?" "Should all of those wires be hanging down?"

Now, mind you, I really enjoy having my better half join me on my automotive sojourns. The problem is the ability she has, and, according to my married buddies, other wives have, to notice things that we don't notice, or choose not to notice. Yes, the tailpipe occasionally vibrates against the frame. It started doing that when I accidentally shifted the car into reverse at 55 miles an hour. Nothing's been the same underneath since that ill-fated twist of the wrist. I have chosen not to notice it and have, as a result, succeeded. Not so when the former Miss Nithart rides shotgun. "Doesn't that noise bother you?" It didn't until she asked.

Then there's the heater situation. The good Lord has, for whatever reason, decided that every car that I shall ever own will have a faulty heater. It either does not work or does not stop working. I deal with an over-zealous heater by rolling down the window. A sweater takes care of any heatless heater. My wife deals with it by saying (you are not going to believe this), "Why don't you fix it?" Can you believe her! If it doesn't bother me, it should not bother anyone else. I just bought a totally restored 1966 Mustang GT. Well, almost totally restored. The heater doesn't work. Maybe now Mrs. Lambert will wear that swell sweater that I bought her for Christmas. The one with, "He loves me almost as much as he loves his Mustang" stitched across the front. She's a beauty. And so is my wife.

Most of the items that she notices are of little consequence. Yes, it would only take me two months of weekends, or a competent mechanic an afternoon, to fix the various problems. But these little faults give the car character. It's like when your favorite T-shirt becomes your favorite workout T-shirt, then T-shirt pajama top, then crawl-under-the-car T-shirt. Yes, it now has a few holes and worn spots, but you feel great wearing it and think it's just fine as it is.

So here's my advice to all of you wives who have made it this far in my rant about my wife's complaining. Wear earplugs, roll the window up or down depending on the interior temperature, enjoy the Shell #5 perfume odor and keep quiet about the banging noise that sounds like a union boss trying to break out of the trunk. Your husband doesn't notice any of it.

Drive-In Delight

Last evening I again experienced one of life's simple pleasures-- the local drive-in restaurant.

It was a warm summer evening and I decided to take full advantage of this quickly diminishing circumstance. Combining the setting sun's warmth with a ride in my 1950 Studebaker Champion seemed like the perfect way to top off my day.

Stately Lambert Manor is located about two miles from a Seattle landmark--the Holman Road Dick's Drive-in. This popular burger palace is always busy, always fun and frequently the destination for collector car enthusiasts. It occasionally now looks the same as it did when many of the old cars parked in the lot were new. The first of several Dick's drive-ins opened in 1954, and I'm sure the various locations have been the brief home to many Studebakers over the years.

My high school years were filled with many afternoons and evenings parked at Tacoma's Frisko Freeze drive-in. Opened in 1950 by Perry Smith, Frisko Freeze looks exactly the same as it did when my 1954 Oldsmobile leaked oil in the parking lot 45 years ago.

My favorite burger joint for the past 20 years has been the Triple XXX drive-in located in Issaquah, WA. They host car shows on 25 weekends a year and there is no other place in the Northwest that can compare when it

comes to '50s and '60s memorabilia. The interior is literally overflowing with items from the past, the plates are overflowing with embarrassingly huge hamburgers and the parking lot on Saturday evenings and Sunday afternoons is frequently overflowing with hot rods, customs and classics. The past few years have shown that the younger "tuner car" crowd also appreciates the XXX's charms.

So here I am, driving the "Studee" to Dick's and wondering what I'll find waiting for me besides a chocolate milkshake. Much to my surprise, there is a 1950 Studebaker pickup parked under the giant Dick's neon sign. It's not unusual to find a classic vehicle parked there, but it is rare to find another Studebaker utilizing some of the drive-in's well traveled asphalt real estate. Sitting in the truck's bed and consuming some fries is a teenager named Jacob. There are two unlikely things happening: two 1950 Studebakers parked in the lot and one of them is owned by a teenager. Most teenagers are driving

foreign cars that outperform old Studebakers and are cheaper to own and operate. Why did Jacob choose to own a truck that is difficult to drive, expensive to maintain and not likely to appeal to his peers?

"I love old trucks and especially old Studebakers," he replied after we introduced ourselves and did the secret Studebaker owner's handshake. He was as surprised as I was to see another Studee glowing under the neon sign and it didn't matter to either of us that I'm old

enough to be his grandfather. What mattered is that we shared the traditional American activity of stopping off at the burger joint to show off our cars, enjoy some high cholesterol bliss and admire the other cars parked nearby. On this evening we were joined by a battalion of BMWs piloted by guys about the right age to be Jacob's big brothers.

These times are trying for all of us and we should find diversions from all of life's challenges. My recommendation is to jump in your car, new or old, drive to the nearest drive-in and carry on the American tradition of biting a burger or consuming a cone, making new friends and seeing the neon splendor reflecting on antique chrome bumpers.

Do you want fries with that?

Road Rage Reflection

I am not a person who is prone to "road rage," but occasionally I will voice my opinion of someone whose driving does not match the unquestionable expertise of my sterling driving ability. This is done in the privacy of my own vehicle and does not include rolling down the window and screaming, "Get off the road, you stinking amateur!" I keep the window rolled up when enthusiastically expressing that opinion.

Occasionally, however, I have been the stinking amateur.

A few years ago I was in Twisp, WA attending a car show with several of my friends. At that time I owned a 1970 Chevrolet C10 pickup that had undergone a lot of modifications, including lower suspension, high performance engine, custom interior, restyled hood and tailgate, shaved doors (door handles removed) and the passenger cab chopped four inches. For those not educated in the custom car world, chopping the cab four inches means four inches are removed from the height of the pickup's cab. The result of this alteration gives it a sleeker, lower and more sinister look. Sinister is generally not good, but many people in the old car hobby think it is very good when it comes to improving the look of a car or truck.

We made the trip to this rural community to attend the car show and enjoy some small town charm. We were staying at a friend's home a couple of miles from Winthrop, another small town located about 10 miles northwest of Twisp. After arriving in

Winthrop on Saturday, we spent the afternoon enjoying a few beers and a lot of laughs. The evening included a BBQ, after which we retired for the night and anticipated the fun we'd be having at the car show the following day.

Early the next morning we arose, dusted off our chariots and headed out for the short drive to the car show. The day started a bit slow for me so I told the others that I'd meet them at the show. I prepared the truck and began the drive to Twisp.

It was then that I met what was presumably the local road warrior.

This inconsiderate guy was suddenly behind me in his Jeep Cherokee. He was so close behind that all I could see in the rearview mirror were his headlights and the top of his hood. What the heck was this guy trying to do, run over the top of my truck? We were on a very narrow strip of roadway, but he could have cautiously passed if the customized Chev pickup in front of him was going too slow.

It was time to take some aggressive action. The bumper hugger behind was about to get one of my deadly stare downs. I was going to purse my lips, furrow my brow, make my eyes all squinty and piercy and then turn, glare at him out of the rear window and, no doubt, fill him with terror. Yes, this aggressive driver behind me was going to have nightmares for weeks in which he saw nothing but my frightening whammy stare.

OK fella, you asked for it.

I turned to give him "the look" and immediately realized that the Jeep was a Washington State Patrol vehicle with the red and blue lights on top twirling in all of their festive and frightful glory. The road warrior behind me was actually a road angel and I was the nitwit who would not get out of his way so he could travel to someone's aid.

The problem, besides the numbskull driving my truck, was that the top of the truck's cab being lowered four inches resulted in the rear window being much smaller than originally designed. This slim rear window restricted the

reflection in the rearview mirror and cut off just enough so that I could only see the front end and hood of the State Patrol officer's Jeep, but not the roof and the emergency lights blinking and blazing.

I pulled over, he sped by and I gave some thought to what had just happened. I wanted to roll down my window and yell an apology but he was long gone.

The look on my face had gone from surly to silly. My apologies to the trooper from Twisp.

Right? Wrong!

Here's the recipe: take an octogenarian, add the low mileage car that he has owned since 1953 and mix in a naive buyer who thinks he knows more about cars than he actually does. Stir this combination and before you know it, you have a buyer baked into a warm humble pie.

I couldn't help myself. This pretty 1952 Chevrolet Styleline two-door sedan had been driven only 30,000 miles since it was sitting on the showroom floor back when Dwight D. Eisenhower was running for president. The dark green beauty had an interesting history and the seller was willing to accept my low offer. I had no choice but to buy the car. Besides, it only needed a small investment of time and money to be perfect. Wrong! It took more time and money than any of the dozens of 1940s through 1960s cars that I've owned.

The first assault upon the Lamberts' miniscule bank account was for a new gas tank. I knew that it needed a new gas tank when the tow truck driver pointed out the severe rust damage to what was left of the existing gas tank. He had been called after the third breakdown caused by rust unsuccessfully trying to make its way through the fuel system.

It's easy to find vendors that sell gas tanks for 1949 to 1951 and 1953 and newer Chevrolets, but not for 1952 Chevrolets. What was so mysterious about the gas tank of a 1952 model? Actually, there is very little difference. After making a lot of calls and asking a lot of questions, I bought the 1951 gas tank. A little modification to the mounting straps resulted in a perfect fit. The cost of the tow truck, plus the gas tank, plus the installation resulted in the fuel properly flowing in the car and the money improperly flowing out of our bank account. Oh well, that was the only major thing I'd have to do, right? Wrong!

The exhaust system leaked, so why not add a split intake manifold and dual exhaust system? I didn't want to pay the prices that local vendors were asking, so out came the *HEMMINGS* catalog. I spent a lot of time and long distance phone charges calling various leads until I found a guy with everything I needed for a reasonable price. This Midwest supplier sold me an exhaust manifold, dual intake manifold, carburetor and chrome valve cover for a 216-cubic-inch engine rather than the 235-cubic-inch engine that I told him was in the car. He refused to refund any money or admit that he had made a mistake. He said that the exhaust guy didn't know what he was doing, the mechanic didn't know what he was doing, the carburetor shop didn't know what they were doing and that the 1952 Chevrolet 216s and 235s had the same valve covers. Wrong!

How about installing a handsome set of rally wheels? That should be easy, right? Wrong! The local vendor selling these wheels had two of the appropriate size in stock and said he could get two more in a few days. One week passed but still only two wheels were available. Two weeks went by but there were still only two wheels in stock. After three weeks he found one more wheel. I decide that he was not actually in the business of selling wheels so I moved on to plan B.

Every automotive swap meet of reasonable size is overflowing with custom wheel sellers. I shared my sad wheel story with a vendor, and he told me that I was being taken by the other vendor. He then said that he would sell me a set of wheels for about half of the previous vendor's price. He just needed to check his supply and then would call me on Monday. Monday passed but he hadn't called. I called him on Thursday and he said that he still needed to check his stock and then would call me back on the following Monday. Again Monday passed with no call so I again called him. He apologized and said that he would call me back on, you guessed it, the following Monday.

The question might be, why did I continue trying to do

business with this wheel bad businessman? Hey, maybe he'd finally come through and I would have saved a significant amount of money.

Another Monday passed so I called him again. A woman answered and said, "He's been trying to reach you. Your number is right here on the refrigerator." At this point I had been sick for two days, most of the time lying on the couch next to the phone. I verified with her that the refrigerator was adorned with the correct number. "Yes, that's the number he's been trying to reach you at." She was very apologetic and said she would have him call me in 20 minutes. Again there was no return call.

My incredible business sense told me that perhaps this guy didn't need my money. I called a local tire vendor and ordered a set of wheels. Two days later they called to let me know that the wheels had arrived. Thank you, First Tire & Wheel!

I ran into the wheel bad businessman at a swap meet a few weeks later. I couldn't walk by his booth without saying something. He angrily responded, "I never said I'd call you!" Fortunately, my limited experience in any form of physical violence stopped me from ripping off this jackass's head. Instead I told him that my new wheels looked great.

Could anything else be as frustrating as my attempts at getting new wheels? Yes.

I needed a 12-volt electrical system on the Chev. It started fine, all of the electrical systems worked properly, but I needed a 12-volt system, right? That's one of the first things we car nuts do, isn't it? Everyone asked me when I was going to convert to a 12-volt system. I couldn't let them down. I hired professionals to do the conversion, paid the bill and drove off. It was a very short drive. The generator went out within a few hours. I called the shop and they said no problem, bring the car back and they'd fix the problem. They fixed it and again I drove off into the sunset. Soon the amp gauge indicated a discharge, and it was not honorable. Back to the shop I went. They fixed the problem and I left thinking that I'd not be returning. No more electrical problems, right? Wrong! The amp gauge again indicated that the Chev's electrical system was not charging. I returned the car to the shop and again the crew attempted to solve the problem. This time they rewired the entire engine compartment and the problem was finally fixed permanently. That was easy, only four trips and the unnecessary 12-volt upgrade was working properly.

OK, now it was time for a little bodywork. Nothing major, just a touchup here and there. While they were at it I had them put on several new pieces of chrome and stainless trim. They also filled in a couple of holes in the hood so the new piece of bull-nose chrome would fit properly. I asked them to take out the grill and paint a couple of the pieces the same green color as the body. They also fixed a couple of small dents in other areas.

The body shop said it would take two weeks at the most. Six weeks later it was finally finished. Well, almost finished. They gave me the painted grill parts so that I could put the re-chromed grill back together. There was one problem; they had painted the grill the wrong color. They acknowledged the mistake and repainted it the right color. I put the grill back together and it looked perfect. The paint was the right color and the new chrome looked great. The grill was flawless and deserved to be in an art gallery. I took it back to the body shop and they installed it. When the car was finally ready I pointed out to them a very new and very large chip in the painted portion of the grill. A week later the shiny and chipless Chev was finally finished.

The car was now running terribly. Something was wrong with the new dual carburetor system. A significant amount of gas was leaking and the dual carburetors seemed to be dueling with each other. Back into the shop she went. One of the risers under one carburetor was cracked. Off I went to track down a new part. A local shop had a set for only five bucks. Five dollars later I learned that the set was the wrong size. Another local shop had a set for twenty bucks. The money was spent and I now owned another set of incorrect sized risers. Another shop, $40 this time and, yes, again the wrong size. I tracked down an ancient mechanic who easily reworked one of the $20 risers and made it fit correctly.

I finally had a fuel system that worked properly and, as a bonus, a lifetime supply of incorrect risers.

The 1952 Chevrolet project went on for several more months. The car also got new brakes, carpeting, sound system, door glass, additional re-chroming, dropped front spindles and dozens of additional "nickel and dime" upgrades.

Am I glad I took on this project? No. Will I ever do it again? No. Did I like the car? Yes; it was gorgeous and I loved it!

213 Pounds of Love

Every year men and women spend days, or perhaps weeks, giving thought to how to best express their love and devotion to their mates. THE day that is best utilized to express this love is Valentine's Day. I'd like to take a few moments of your time to share with you what my wife's reaction might be when she receives (tomorrow as I write this) this year's expression of my deepest feelings for her.

Some people feel that a simple card decorated with hearts is sufficient. Others spend large amounts of time and money acquiring or creating just the right expression of love. I fall into the latter category, and, as you will learn, perhaps will set a new standard at the Lambert home for the sincere communication of love.

None of the standard gifts will do: flowers, candy, a night on the town, flower petals leading to the bedroom, ah...and some other stuff. No, this year is going to be special. This year's gift of love is tall and sturdy, able to be both open and welcoming and closed and protective. Also, according to the manufacturer, it weighs 213 pounds. No, it is not a slightly overweight but still handsome soap opera star; it's (get ready ladies, you are about to squeal with delight and envy) a new storage shed! I can hear you say, "Why couldn't I have been so lucky as to marry a guy like him?"

Can you imagine Mrs. Lambert's excitement when she learns that, rather than flowers that will soon reside in the yard waste bin, or an expensive meal that will add inches to her waistline, she will be the proud co-owner of the best storage shed that $400 can buy. And the only storage shed that $400 can buy. She will care not that the walls are the same thickness as a tinfoil gum wrapper. Nor will she care that the "takes only three hours to build" instructions mean that it will take two to three days to screw all of the pieces together (longer if any trips to the beer cooler, emergency ward, or both are required). And upon completion we will no longer need to have any more "discussions" concerning whether or not a lawn mower or five bicycles belong in the garage. Every bicycle that is taking up floor space (I don't ride a bike and she can only ride one at a time) is less floor space for important garage stuff like old cars, old gas pumps and old pedal cars. No longer will my car buddies' paths to the well stocked refrigerator be impeded by having to climb over unused camping gear and boxes of unknown relatives' photographs. Finally the garage will be utilized for its intended purpose--unobstructed gatherings of car guys telling embellished stories, consuming healthy food (beer, chips, beer, salsa, beer and beer) and sprawling upon furniture that, in a previous life, was the major portion of a 1958 Rambler station wagon's interior. I shudder with excitement in anticipation of her glee upon trying to open a large cardboard box that weighs 213 pounds. No doubt she will throw her arms around me and exclaim, "Oh darling, how did you know that all I wanted for Valentine's Day is for you to have more room in the garage for your stuff!?"

In over 32 years she's never called me "Darling," but I think that is about to change. I wonder what else she will call me?

T-Bird Tears

A few friends accuse me of being too attached to my old cars. They are correct.

Many years ago I attended the Portland Swap Meet with the intent of coming home with four tires attached to a really great car. I didn't have any particular car in mind, just one that tugged at my heart and needed a new home. The search was very successful.

There, parked at the swap meet, was the most beautiful 1960 Thunderbird that I had ever seen. This bright red and white "squarebird" was as nice, or nicer, than the day it was sitting brand new at a Portland Ford dealership. It had recently undergone a complete restoration that included the interior, exterior, engine and all mechanical systems. The restoration, enhanced by chrome wire wheels, made this car stunning.

The term "squarebird" refers to 1958, 1959 and 1960 T-Birds. They have a distinctive squared off style, due to the fins and body sculpturing, and slightly resemble the Caped Crusader's Batmobile.

I struck a deal with the seller and away I drove in my new old car.

That night I sat on the steps of my motel room and stared at the Thunderbird. I am not embarrassed to admit that I was so struck with the beauty of the car that a few tears began to flow. Readers not passionate about their cars, new or old, will be confused by this reaction. Car lovers will understand. The tears were the result of appreciating the car's breathtaking design as the paint and chrome sparkled under the glow of the motel's neon sign.

Eight years of ownership passed during which time the car appeared at over 100 car shows. It was appreciated by car show attendees and, more than once I heard the remark, "I usually don't care much for 'squarebirds,' but I sure like yours." It brought home an occasional trophy, carried the family on several great sojourns and ended most days looking pretty as it rested in the garage. It never broke down, always caressed its occupants in luxury, and glided down the road like a true bird.

I loved the car, but, after eight years, the T-Bird's glamour was beginning to fade and the cost of refurbishing was not in my budget. It was time to allow someone else to be the car's caretaker. I advertised it for sale and waited for a new owner to enter the squarebird's life. It didn't take long. I made a sale and the new owner said she would pick up the car the following day.

That evening I told my wife Jan that I was going to the garage to say goodbye to the T-Bird. I opened the car door and climbed into the driver's seat. Then it happened; much to my surprise I began bawling. Not just a few tears or a good cry but a racking, sobbing blubberfest. I felt like I was saying a final goodbye to one of my closest friends or relatives. Clearly, I wasn't handling the farewell very well. But it was too late to reconsider the sale and, after eight years, it was time to move on to the stewardship of a different new old car.

The following day the new owner drove off to write the Thunderbird's next chapter. I didn't shed any additional tears. Instead I felt sadness combined with best wishes for the T-Bird's future.

I guess I'm still a bit attached to that car.

Ugly Eighties?

My wife and daughter no longer have any respect for me. They also think I'm nuts.

Over the past few years I've taken an interest in American cars of the 1980s. This may be due to too much tofu in my diet, eating lead bicycle paint as a child or having grown up in Tacoma. Whatever the cause, it's there--an appreciation of cars that are not really old but are definitely no longer "newer." The 1988 Pontiac Fiero GT I recently purchased is a good example. This car is in excellent condition, mid-life crisis red, and best of all, cheap. For less

than the cost of a week's vacation I have a flashy go-kart that gets me from point A to point B in fun style. The design has encouraged a few of the vehicle-challenged to ask, "Is that a Ferrari?" It causes my daughter enough embarrassment to result in her never asking me to give her a ride anywhere, and my wife never asks to borrow "that" car.

The Fiero soon had a garage mate when I saw a 1988 Saleen Mustang for sale at a very reasonable price. It seems that the seller had some law enforcement problems that resulted in his need to immediately sell the car.

Saleen Mustangs are Mustangs that race-car builder Steve Saleen modifies by adding racing suspension, heavy duty brake system, high performance engine tuning, custom interiors and other

"hey, don't mess with me if you know what's good fer ya" modifications.

My wife's reaction when I arrived home with Steve's creation was, "I'm going to have to trust you on this one." Our daughter, never at a loss

187

for words, reacted with a heartwarming, "Daaaaaad, that looks like the kind of car a drunken 16-year-old kid would get arrested in!" How dare she say such a thing; the seller was at least 20 years old.

Recently, my daughter and I were returning from dropping off her much cooler, by her standards, Saab for repairs when we passed a 1987 Cadillac Allante. I commented that I thought they were beautifully designed cars and my daughter went a bit crazy on me. "Daaaaaad, that car is really ugly! What has happened to you? You used to only buy really cool cars from the 1950s and now you are buying these awful cars from the 1980s." These remarks are coming from someone who drives a Saab, a car that is a pleasure to drive as long as you are of Swedish descent and enjoy driving a car that has every switch, dial and gizmo in the wrong place. I relayed this incident to my wife, who immediately chimed in that she fully agreed with Saab Girl and wanted to know if my years of collector-car exhaust exposure have resulted in some sort of right brain malfunction.

Here's the way I see it; an interesting American car manufactured in the 1980s is cheap ($3000 to $6000 for the best one in the state), plentiful (drive by any really used used car lot and take your pick) and very unlikely to be stolen by anyone.

I have not heard that Saabs are a hot item in the grand theft auto community either.

The "Y" Word

It is six o'clock in the evening and a bunch of people are in my garage. There are 15 crew members, two food service workers, a director and three actors. I should have known better.

Production vehicles are up and down my street and a huge truck is in my driveway. My newly acquired 1952 Chevrolet has been cast out into the street. My 1960 Thunderbird has been put up on car stands so that a 300-pound actor can get under it – a 300 pound actor dressed in a Shakespearean outfit and pretending to be working on the bottom of the T-Bird with a saber.

I was asked to take down my very large Studebaker dealership sign so they could put up an even larger piece of lighting equipment. I had to ask the neighbor kid to stop shooting hoops and two neighbor girls to stop rollerblading because of the noise.

The crew arrived at 7 a.m. and I was just informed that the shooting is going to continue until at least midnight. They are appreciative but have also let me know that the less I'm around the more they will appreciate it. The sound engineer is extremely demanding and gives me the impression that he is a descendant of someone who was very high up in the Third Reich leadership.

What did I do to deserve this misery? I made a fatal mistake; I uttered the word "yes."

I'm sworn to secrecy as to the script, but I'll give you a hint. It's a Shakespearean style comedy, taking place in modern times about a teenager having difficulty getting through puberty. It sounds like a film that many of us have starred in. It's based on a screenplay, titled "Speare," written by actor, comedian and musician Ken Boynton. Ken and I are good friends, and when he saw the size of my garage I became his even better friend. He asked if the film company could spend a day utilizing my garage and Thunderbird for a few scenes. That's when I made the mistake previously mentioned-- the one where I said the "Y" word.

Hosting my TV program, the *Vintage Vehicle Show*, frequently results in me being the guy imposing on other people's lives and property when I successfully trick them into saying the "Y" word. The difference is my crew usually consists of only two or three camera operators, producer Tim Stansbury and me. We are very fast, due to having a budget of about three bucks per episode.

Alas (I can use that word since the film is done in Shakespearean style), I'm resigned to just sit it out and let this mob have its way with my garage and car. It will make me feel justified the next time I try to trick a person into saying the "Y" word.

EPILOGE: The short film, titled *Much Ado About Puberty*, went on to win a few awards and was broadcast on various television outlets. It was one of a three part series parodying various Shakespearean plays.

Grins in the Garage

"There's a lot of testosterone in this garage!"

This comment was made by my friend and neighbor Karen when she walked into her garage and listened to the exchanges going on between her husband Joe and several of the neighborhood car guys. Joe had asked us to come over and help him place the newly painted Factory 5 Cobra body on the chassis of the car that he's been building for the past three years.

Several things seem to happen whenever car guys gather together: joking and good natured teasing begins, old stories are re-told and best of all, laughter fills the room. The right combination of participants usually results in a raging river of wit, or at least the perception by the participants that everyone in the room is incredibly witty.

I'm not sure if Karen thought we were witty or just a bunch of Joe's friends being goofy. I think we were likely a combination of both, but I'm not sure that testosterone was the common ingredient.

In my circle of friends the most important goal at any gathering is to make others laugh. We will use all of the laughter ammunition available: a good natured tease or insult here, a joke or story from the past there, and plays on words and innuendos everywhere. It's why my friends have become my friends.

The world that I live in is immersed in the culture of the automobile. Most of my friends and associates are car guys, most of my activities are within the old car hobby, I make my living by producing and hosting a TV show about old cars and, thank goodness, I'm married to a wonderful woman who encourages my passion for old cars. But are old cars the most important part of the hobby? No, it's the people and the laughter that make most car guy gatherings a comedy show.

It's likely that golfers, square dancers, musicians, bowlers and every other hobby community feels the same way. Laughter is the best medicine in this angry world, and everyone should consider taking every opportunity to be a pharmacist dispensing the medicine of laughter.

So there we are early on a Saturday morning, waiting for Joe's direction on how best to remove the Cobra body from the support stand, lift it over the chassis and gently park it in place without scratching the shiny new black paint.

Immediately comments began flying:

"Shouldn't we have a few beers first?"

"My back has been acting up so I'll let you guys take care of this."

"Where are the snacks? Shouldn't there be a table of snacks?"

"Is this scratch supposed to be here?"

"Hey, it's not my car. So what if it gets scratched."

"It's 10:30. Is it time to break for lunch yet?"

This incredibly high level of intellectual wit continued until the Cobra body was properly placed on the chassis and the common goal of helping Joe while making him and others laugh had been accomplished. Every wisecrack was delivered and received as a gift between friends.

Karen was helping and laughing too, but perhaps her testosterone observation was incorrect. The definition of testosterone includes, among other things, "used to prepare for confrontations" and "causes noticeable strength and aggressiveness."

On second thought...

Pedal Passion

My wife's husband is turning into Peewee Herman.

Lately I've taken an interest in old bicycles, mainly those manufactured in the 1940s through the 1960s. I'm not sure why; it just happened. There are already five bicycles in my home, none of which I ever ride. Jan, my bride of 36 years, occasionally dusts off one of our aging ten-speed spindly butt busters and pedals along one of the local bike paths that dissect Seattle. Upon her return she says how much she enjoyed the ride and then returns all ten speeds to the bicycle menagerie. A year or two later this adventure and comment is repeated. I have little interest in participating in the ride because it just seems like too much bother.

Why is it that I do not care about jaunts on one of our toothpick framed multi-speed high-tech contraptions but, instead, have taken a strong interest in old clunky dinosaur contraptions that are heavy, bulky and a bit silly looking?

When I was very young, about 8 years old, I became the owner of a brand new Schwinn Black Phantom bicycle. To the uninformed reader this may mean nothing. To the informed reader (you know who you are, you began moaning in ecstasy at the words Black Phantom), this is the Holy Grail of bicycles of that era. It was huge, heavy, gaudy and the most expensive bicycle manufactured by Schwinn at the time. The informed also know that an average sized 8-year-old boy and a Schwinn Black Phantom don't mesh very well. That black and red beauty was too big and too heavy for me to ride, so it sat parked in the basement waiting for me to acquire a few more pounds and inches. After a couple of years I was ample enough in physical stature to control that rhinoceros of a bicycle.

The acquisition of the bicycle still remains a bit of a mystery. My father told me that he bailed a friend out of jail and, to show his appreciation, the recently sprung jail cell dweller gave the bike to my dad. I have a strong suspicion that the bike "fell off the back of a truck" or came from some other dubious origin. I didn't care where it came from, and, instead, cared that I now owned the coolest bike on Tacoma's Junett Street. As mentioned, I got bigger and the bike got ridden.

After a few years bicycles were no longer desirable to me and they were eventually replaced by four-wheeled contraptions that were less reliable than my Black Phantom.

Pedal fast forward to the recent past and you will find me paying renewed attention to old bikes. I think some of the interest was spawned by the Peewee Herman movie "Peewee's Big Adventure," where perpetual child Peewee tries to find his stolen bicycle. Mr. Herman's bike was a custom-made bicycle that started out as a late-forties Schwinn frame that was then over-accessorized to the point of being a parody of "tankers" of the period.

Tankers had the appearance of having a gas tank between the seat and handlebars, with the tank frequently housing a push-button horn. Peewee's bike had lights, multiple horns, saddlebags, full fenders, carrying rack and a dozen or more additional options and accessories popular during the 1940s to the early 1960s. These overdone bikes appeal to me not only because they are comfortable to ride, but because they are now viewed as both a bit eccentric and a bit unusual. They were typical American design for the period--short on practicality and long on overdone.

My re-education about old bicycles consisted of reading online and print histories of various bikes, watching auction results and talking to a couple of bike collector friends who knew a good bike from a bad bike and a good buy from a bad buy. I was told about an upcoming bike swap meet and marked the date on the calendar. At 7:00 a.m. on the swap meet day I began roaming the rows of bike parts, carcasses and pedal-power memorabilia. The "tankers" were not plentiful and those that I found were either totally worn-out disasters with very high prices or beautiful bikes with prices in the thousands of dollars.

Then I spotted MY new-old bike.

The second choice on my bike bucket list was a Schwinn Sting Ray. These are small bikes that were introduced by the Schwinn company in 1963 and ranged from stripped down basic bikes to over-accessorized models to which the manufacturer did everything possible to make riders think they were straddling a chopper motorcycle or driving a hot-rod Corvette. The Sting Rays at the swap meet were more reasonably priced than tankers and would not require a second mortgage on our home. A Sting Ray is not a tanker, but it is a step closer to getting one.

I purchased a 1969 Schwinn Sting Ray for a very reasonable price. It's an original basic model with the exception of a very well done new paint on the frame and forks. It has no accessories but does have the very cool "banana" seat and "ape hanger" high-rise handle bars. I am hoping that this Sting Ray will be followed by a true tanker style bike in the future.

Perhaps Jan will be accompanied on her next bicycle ride by Peewee Lambert.

Shag Carpeting and Fresh Eggs

In the recent past I was the proud owner of a 1970 Chevrolet C10 pickup that was not your typical farmer Brown manure hauler. It was an award winner that never transported anything other than the owner and his "finance manager." The top was chopped four inches lower; the body featured a custom hood, doors and tailgate, and the whole thing was dropped five inches closer to the terra firma. The original engine had been replaced with a high-performance-built 350-cubic-inch motor, and the interior had been turned into a tasteful replica of an upscale brothel (I've seen them in the movies). That truck was definitely a vehicle made for car shows, and not for hauling the pet pig to the county fair or sheetrock for the kitchen remodel.

There are some among you who may question the wisdom of making all of these modifications to such a utilitarian vehicle, or making any modifications to any car or truck. Perhaps a better question is why do some car lovers think that they are smarter than the entire design staffs of Ford, General Motors, Chrysler and dozens of other companies that decide what our next car will look like? One answer is that these corporate designers, despite all of their experience, fail on occasion. Have you ever taken a look at a Pontiac Aztec? The design department's water cooler was definitely filled with bad hallucinogens the day they decided that the Aztec design was a good idea. Another answer is that some car lovers, like chefs, can't leave well enough alone. Who decided that it was a good idea to put pineapple on a pizza?

The other side of the coin is that the car hobby is full of cars that perhaps should have been left in their original configuration. Custom car icons, such as "King of the Kustomizers" George Barris, have built many beautiful cars, but also some horrible cars. The late Ed "Big Daddy" Roth, a man justifiably sitting on a very high pedestal, built a car that, thankfully, self-destructed from the weight of its own body modifications. Some people, or at least two or three, thought that the AMC Pacer was a great looking car. Others think that it was an eyesore and was the last nail in AMC's coffin. In the 1970s one car hobbyist thought that installing orange shag carpeting and disco lights in his Ford Econoline van was the height of good design. Another thought that putting 1953 Buick side trim on his chopped 1950 Mercury was a good idea. The van is now the home of a flock of chickens and the Mercury just sold for $85,000. Somebody got it right and somebody else has fresh eggs every day.

A good example of successful corporate design was the first Mustang. The early release date of the 1965 Mustang set the automotive world on fire. Here was a crisply designed mid-sized automobile that, despite being a Falcon in a pretty dress, convinced grocery clerks and accountants that they could feel like Sterling Moss for a very reasonable price. The design was simple but a bit daring and, as proved by Ford's sales charts, immensely appealing to the market. Not many buyers decided to make changes to a car that was already well designed.

The Chrysler Corporation crew's design choices with the 1965 Plymouth Barracuda proved to be not quite so successful. What should have had the same appeal as the Mustang, in fact, did not. Both were mid-sized cars that had a long hood, a short trunk and sporty design. But while the Mustang looked sleek and simple, the Barracuda resembled a fish bowl. No bottles of champagne were opened at the Chrysler headquarters in celebration of Barracuda sales.

The average Joe, recognizing a good design, bought a new Mustang and made no alterations. The other Joe down the street waited a short time until the Barracuda was a reasonably priced used car and then purchased it, lowered it, changed the interior, made a few changes to the body and applied a custom paint job. Presto: a car that now appealed to the owner and many other car hobbyists.

Perhaps this proves that the average car lover is capable of both recognizing a car that should be left as originally designed and knowing when a car needs some help.

Now, if you will excuse me, I have to run to the store. They are having a sale on shag carpeting.

To Build of Not to Build

There are three types of individuals in the old car hobby: a little crazy, a lot crazy and totally crazy. Their level of craziness may be determined by how they acquired their special-interest car, be it a hot rod, original/stock or classic.

The first method is to find some old iron in need of restoration or altering, drag it home, shove it in the garage, convince your spouse and children that you have not lost your mind, and then proceed to take the next one to 20 years "fixing it up." This has to be done while defending your decision to your family, friends and neighbors. Some will commend you for following your dream of bringing a derelict car back to new condition. Others will think that you are crazy. Both of these perspectives are correct.

One good thing about this choice is that you get the pleasure of creating beauty out of rust and rot. You will become a better craftsperson and be filled with pride when your project is completed, assuming it ever gets completed. For many hobbyists, the "build" of an old car is the best part of the old car hobby. Hundreds of evenings and weekends in the garage will be filled with the pleasure of cleaning, grinding, sanding, screwing, fitting, sanding, pounding, cussing and sanding. Upon completion you will drive past your friends' and neighbors' homes while revving up your sputtering four banger, or belching V8, and yelling, "I did it! I did it." Your spouse may also be proud of you, unless your years of hiding in the garage have resulted in you being a participant in a weekly singles gathering. Some good advice is to not mention your love of working on old cars to any potential future partner.

The second method is to take the same rusting hulk to a restoration or custom shop and, over the next one to five years, give them enormous amounts of money to do the work that you have chosen not to do yourself. Your spouse may not agree that the money is being well spent and other people may think that you are crazy. Both of these perspectives are also correct.

The bonus of having professionals do the "build" is that they are just that, professionals. The other possibility is that they may not be, despite what the sign on the building says, professionals. Many cars have to be "re-restored" or "re-customized" as a result of a car owner choosing the wrong person to give the monthly bag of money to under the illusion that the builder is a professional. The car hobby is full of participants who have given 75K to 200K to shops and, in return, are given back cars that are worth 30K to 50K. Hey, if you have the money and time, then go for it! If not, then read the next paragraph.

The third method is to find a completed or original car in good condition, buy it and begin playing with your new toy immediately. This manner of acquiring a special-interest car is considered by some to be the most sensible and quickest way to enjoy the pleasure of having the car that you lusted for in your youth but couldn't afford. The downside is that you didn't build it yourself and are denied the pleasure of enjoying a car that is truly your creation. The upside is that there is still enough money in your wallet to pay for the other necessary items in your family's life. You may also have to endure the insult of being called a "checkbook mechanic." The person making this comment may be the same person who, for the past 15 years, has had a rusting hulk sinking into the back yard as it waits to be "fixed up."

In 2008 I purchased a beautiful 1940 Plymouth coupe that was a total frame-off restoration. The previous owner spent four years doing the rotisserie restoration. He did most of the work himself but still spent over $30,000. I purchased the car from his estate for $10,000.

There certainly are worse ways to spend your dollars and time, but what better way than on these four-wheeled chariots of the gods. How crazy you want to be is up to you.

Reunion Passion

It's been forty years but I'm still in love with her.

A few weeks ago I had the great pleasure of attending my high school's 40th reunion. Tacoma's Stadium High School's class of 1965 was a great group back then and remains a great group to spend time with at our reunions.

I was looking forward to seeing certain people, when someone special that I didn't expect to see walked into the room. This vision of beauty took my breath away.

I was mingling with some classmates and laughing about our teenage misadventures when "she" walked into the room. I was totally unable to act casual or conceal my excitement. I gazed in amazement and then ran across the room to throw my arms around her. I can't begin to express how great she felt and, yes, even how good she smelled. Her warmth and softness brought back memories of our cruising together during our teenage years. I had spent so many hours snuggled up tight with her in my 1948 Chev as the car wandered down the street with its bad front suspension. She often hugged me while we rode in my 1954 Olds with its worn out and burping exhaust system. She kept me warm on cool nights, and being

seen with her definitely raised my status in the local hot rod community.

She looked great but was showing her age--frayed at the edges, a few stains here and there, a few repairs and her original royal blue color a bit faded. I barely noticed; she was as beautiful as the day I met her. "She" was an original Steeds Car Club jacket and she still made my pulse race. She was being worn by my friend Loren Ezell, a past member of the club who, like me, just can't grow up and stop dwelling on how much fun the Steeds were and how great we all looked in those matching club jackets. Each jacket had our name on the front and the club's logo on the back--a blown Chrysler Hemi engine with a snorting horse's head coming out the front. It was great remembering when 15 to 20 guys wearing these club jackets got together every Monday for our weekly meeting.

Our Steeds jackets weren't the greaser type that you see in old juvenile delinquent movies; they were a very "Ivy League" style, like what you'd expect to see the Kingston Trio wearing. On some occasions we'd even wear white shirts and ties under our jackets.

I tried to talk Loren into selling me his jacket but he was not willing to give up it up at any price.

I spent the rest of the evening admiring that high school beauty from across the room and dreaming of once again having my own Steeds Car Club jacket to wear.

Patina or Pooh?

One of my favorite ways to waste time is perusing "for sale" ads in various collector-car print and online publications. Doing this since my early teenage years has helped me form some opinions on how prospective buyers can avoid fruitless trips to inspect antique, collector or special interest cars that turn out to be something other than what was advertised. Here are a few pointers on what to watch for when looking for a car.

NO PRICE LISTED – Move on to the next ad as quickly as possible. Not listing the price means that the seller knows nobody will call if the ridiculous sales price is posted.

"CALL FOR MORE INFORMATION" – This is the same as above but with the added unpleasant conversation that includes, "Well, what would you be willing to pay?" or, "The sales manager is out right now and I'm not sure what the price is. Why don't you come on down and take a look."

"NO TIRE KICKERS OR LOOKILOOS" – The seller is very crabby, lives in a house with bars on the windows and only comes out to yell at you for parking in front of his house. He or she also considers anyone who disagrees with the asking price to be a "tire kicker."

"PRICE LOWERED" – Yes, and now it's only overpriced by 50%.

"EITHER I SELL IT TODAY OR IT'S GOING TO THE JUNKYARD" – It belongs in the junkyard.

"LOW MILEAGE CAR!" – Numerous times I've followed up on some of these ads only to find that the advertised car has 100,000 to 150,000 miles on it. The seller's explanation is usually, "It was driven only an average of 7,000 miles a year. Isn't that low mileage?"

"FULLY RESTORED" – This comment nearly resulted in my committing a major felony. I made a 100-mile roundtrip to look at a "fully restored" 1952 Pontiac." On the phone the seller stated, "Yes, it has a new interior." The upholstery was spray-painted silver. No, not reupholstered, just spray-painted. The seller's comment, after I strongly expressed my opinion about his deception, was, "Well, I got you here didn't I." A jury of my "peers" would not convict me for murder had I strangled this twit.

Fully restored means the car is as good as it was on the day the first owner drove it off the lot.

"NO RUST" – Here's the biggy, folks. If the car is advertised as having no rust, it has some rust. If it's advertised as having a little rust, then it has a lot of rust. If it's advertised as needing rust repair (bless the seller for being honest), then it is a total rust bucket that will require you to get a tetanus shot after you've inspected the car.

"SHOW WINNER" – I don't care how crappy your car is; if you enter it in enough shows, you'll eventually bring home a trophy. A friend once won the "Least likely to make it home from the show" award for her 1959 Chevrolet. Fortunately, she and the car made it home. I once attended a show where the show's producer stood in front of the audience and awarded himself two trophies! His "show winner" 1956 Ford looked like it had been painted with a trowel.

Several years ago I bought a car that had a "First Place" award proudly displayed on the front seat. After purchasing the car I learned that the seller had gone to a trophy shop and bought the award.

"BARN FIND" – This is the latest rage in selling old cars. The fantasy is that it is a car in excellent condition despite the heavy layer of dust and the stack of boxes on the roof. The reality is that it's a total piece of junk that was banished to the "barn" for a good reason. "It ran great when I parked it in 1972." Trust me, it does not "run great" anymore.

"PATINA" – This formerly seldom-used word has jumped out of Webster's Dictionary and landed in a lot of ads. The seller wants you to envision a car that is in good condition and has, like antique furniture and Clint Eastwood's face, taken on a look of character and dignity only attained with age. What patina actually means is the car needs everything--paint, interior and all mechanicals repaired or replaced. Webster's defines patina as "a surface appearance of something grown beautiful, especially with age or use." Is the car with patina "beautiful" or just a worn-out car?

"MINT CONDITION" – A car is in mint condition when it is new or has undergone an extensive restoration.

A seller once described his 1963 Studebaker Avanti to me as being in mint condition. Upon close inspection the carpeting actually disintegrated between my fingers. A large, oddly shaped hole had been cut into the dash with the only explanation from the seller being, "Oh that, I don't know why that is there." I had driven 70 miles in Friday traffic to see this "mint" car.

Fresh paint over rust bubbles is not found on a mint car, though I've found this deception on dozens of cars described as being in "mint condition."

These examples are just a few from a long list of "buyer beware" red flags. Dozens of collector cars have been parked in my garage for the past 50 years, and a few, unfortunately, were purchased as a result of me not taking my own advice.

I have to end this article due to a previous commitment. I found an ad for a car that was owned by a preacher and used exclusively for trips to the store and church. No price is listed but I'm sure I can get it cheap.

Fortunate Five

If you could relive a day from your life, what day would you choose?

I was watching a television program about the meaning of Thornton Wilder's play "Our Town." The reporter dwelled on the question of what day in a person's life, if given the opportunity, would be chosen to relive? I rummaged through my memories and tried to raise to the top a memory of my high school girlfriend, a special family event or any specific day that was truly meaningful. What formed before my memory's eyes instead was a simple day often lived.

We all have special friends as we go through life, and, for many, the friends from our youth will always own a piece of our hearts. Four pieces of my heart belong to four very special friends-- Bob, Darrol, Greg and Doug. I'd met them individually in grade school and junior high school. We gradually got to know each other and formed that first ring of friends in the ripples of friendships that surround each of us. These guys were part of my day to relive.

On a Saturday morning I'd give Bob a call and ask what he was doing. "Nothing. Come on over," he'd say. I'd drive my '54 Oldsmobile to his house and receive a warm welcome from his mom as she sent me upstairs to Bob's room.

He and I would sit in his room, look at car magazines, bring some special car to the other's attention and then decide it was time to turn to the next page in our day. "I wonder what Greg and Doug are doing?" We'd call and arrange to meet them at Frisko Freeze, the local drive-in restaurant that we visited seven days a week. Another call would be made to Darrol saying, "We're all meeting at the Freeze. Want to join us?"

A half hour later we'd be doing what we all did the best-- nothing. Parked in the lot would be Bob's 1940 Chev, Greg's 1956 Chev, Doug's 1955 Chev, Darrol's 1938 Chev and my 1954 Olds.

 We'd hang around the parking lot and give each other a good-natured bad time, laugh, find excuses to talk to girls, laugh, talk about someone's car, laugh and then turn to the next page in our day.

"Let's go to Owens Beach!" That's all it took for the five cars and drivers to head to one of the most popular gathering places for Tacoma's teenagers. Owens Beach, located in Point Defiance Park, was a frequent destination for Stadium and Wilson high school students. The beach and the Puget Sound view were beautiful and, best of all, it had a very large parking lot to show off our cars. The parking lot was very close to the water and was the favorite view of the sun bathers. Yes, the parking lot, not the water. The skinny and mostly innocent teenagers actually lay on their blankets facing the parking lot rather than the water. It was more important to see who was cruising by on the asphalt than on the waves.

 Each group of friends had a favorite area to park and that's where the five of us parked our cars and continued teasing each other, laughing and flirting with the girls. We were at the beach but our shoes rarely touched a grain of

sand. The asphalt was our recreational area of choice.

Time would comfortably pass and we'd consider our options for the remainder of the day. A chorus of "I'm going home to have some dinner. Do you want to meet back at the Freeze tonight?" would be sung and we'd cruise out of the park together and then go our separate ways

home. An hour or two later we'd be enjoying the evening's continuation of the day's activities.

Yes, things like school, families and jobs frequently disrupted the easy flow of our day, but, fortunately, the five of us found many opportunities to enjoy turning a day's page together to see what was next in the story of our lives.

This is the day that I'd choose to relive.

Video Vehicles

A television commercial for a local bank currently features footage of my 1950 Studebaker parking at a local drive-in restaurant. This is the third time one of my cars has been turned into a "video vehicle."

Many years ago a movie called "Waiting for the Light" was filmed in the Seattle area. The movie, starring Shirley MacLaine and Teri Garr, was about two women inheriting a diner in 1962. The film's transportation director contacted a club that I belonged to and asked if we could provide some vehicles for use in the film. It sounded like fun and even paid a whopping $80 and a meal for anyone who brought their car to the filming. At the time, I owned a 1954 Ford sedan that had been restored and looked almost new. It was an appropriate car, since many 1954 Fords were still on the road during the film's era. During the filming, most of the club's cars were parked along Seattle's Pioneer Square intersection of First and Jackson streets. This location was perfect because the architecture in this area still looks like 1962.

My Ford was chosen to drive down the street, stop at the light as Teri Garr passed in front of it and then proceed when the light turned green. Before the scene's filming started I was able to spend some time chatting with Teri and was impressed when she asked, "This is a 1954 Ford, right?" She said that during her childhood the family car was a 1954 Ford. It was a fun experience, the $80 was appreciated and the steak and lobster lunch was quickly devoured by me and the other members of the 1949 to 1959 Ford Owners Association.

The movie was entertaining but was a financial flop. Perhaps this was due in part to the title, "Waiting for the Light." At the time, Shirley MacLaine was subject to a lot of criticism because of her spiritual and metaphysical beliefs. The movie title and her name on the marquee may have turned ticket buyers away.

The second opportunity to have a car featured in a movie was for "House of the Rising." It was filmed mostly in Seattle's Capitol Hill neighborhood and featured a cast of unknown actors. The Internet Movie Database describes it as "a psychedelic ensemble drama set at a '60s retro party."

My biased opinion is that the movie's best scene was when a beautiful 1960 T-Bird cruised down a long hill and parked in front of a house where a wild party was taking place. The script called for the two actors to get out of the car while in the middle of an argument.

They yelled at each other across the top of the car, but all I could see was the anti-freeze dripping from the radiator due to the numerous takes required and my T-Bird's inadequate cooling system.

"House of the Rising" went directly to video release, where it died a quiet death.

So there I am on a sunny 2012 spring day cruising to the drive-in to get a burger and a little exercise for the Studebaker. To my surprise, a film crew is there setting up equipment, and it is obvious that this is a "real" film crew. They have top quality professional gear and the crew is large enough that there are a few people standing around with clipboards trying to look like they are doing something important.

"What are you filming?" I asked. "We are doing a documentary about drive-ins around the country," was the reply. I volunteered the use of my 1950 Studebaker and they accepted the offer. They asked me to drive into the parking lot, park and then get out of the car. They did two "takes" and the second take caused one of the camera operators to utter the cliché, "That's the money shot." They had me sign a release, said thank you and sent me on my way. There was no lobster or even a burger offered.

A few visits to the production company's web site did not result in any information about a drive-in documentary being produced. I expected to be part of a warm and fuzzy Ken Burns-style documentary on traditional American drive-ins. Instead the

Studebaker and I end up in a commercial for a bank. The worst part is that the bank being promoted is a bank where I had recently closed out two accounts due to their lousy service.

At least they could have bought me a burger.

Trophyitus

There's a rampant decease raging through the car community that is leaving very few hobbyists uninfected--trophyitus. Signs of infection are many: only attending car shows where your car may have a chance of winning a trophy, looking over the show's entry form and deciding which category has the least competition, repeatedly walking up to the trophy display to decide which trophy you may go home with, patiently waiting for your name to be called during the awards presentation and, finally, after the show arguing with the judges over the fact that your 1962 Super Grand Prix Master Machismo JKLMNOP is much better than the car that beat you in your class. In fact, it's the best damn car in the show!

You, my friend, are fully infected with the trophyitus disease. Unfortunately I speak from experience.

Several years ago I attended a show in a small town located 50 miles northwest of Seattle. I was driving a fully restored 1960 T-Bird that usually took first place honors in Thunderbird shows and occasionally brought home a gold-plated plastic trophy from mixed-brand car shows. This day's show was sure to result in another plastic trophy to place in the most sacred room in any home--the garage. Also in my favor was that it was a miserable day. It was raining cats, dogs, sheep and cows. It was really bad and I was really happy. Nobody in their right mind was going to take their cherished set of wheels out into this mess.

So there I sat all day long in this miserable downpour waiting for the awards presentation. Here's the real clincher; there were nine trophies being awarded and only ten soggy cars and ten soggy car owners participating in the show.

Most car shows end early when the weather is this bad, but not on this day. I did my best to fill seven hours by chatting with my fellow trophyitus sufferers, taking inventory at the local hardware store, spending a little money at a thrift shop, and then returning to the hardware store to make sure I didn't miss anything on the first trip. The community center provided companionship when I struck up a conversation with the very friendly group of ladies who were working on a large quilt. These activities were all going to be worth the time and effort because there was no doubt that I'd return home accompanied by a gigantic 7-inch tall gold-plated plastic and simulated wood-veneer-covered trophy.

Finally the time had arrived--trophy time. I couldn't lose. Four or five of my competitors had cars as good as or better than mine, but the remainder were destined to be residing in wrecking yards in the near future. This was it. It was Miller time. I was about to get a hole in one. I'd successfully grab the golden ring. The Holy Grail was mine. I would win the Oscar. Every cliché' came to mind as I prepared for my victorious walk up to receive my award along with thunderous applause, or at least polite applause from 9 other people.

All of the cars comparable to mine received trophies. The show's organizer and trophy presenter then proudly presented himself with two trophies for his own car! I couldn't believe it. There I stood without a trophy in either hand and he had one in both of his hands. No thunderous applause, no new dust collector to display in the garage, no victorious drive home in the pouring rain.

At that moment a couple of neurons connected in my brain and helped me realize what a silly twit I'd been that day. I also changed my attitude about trophies. Yes, getting a trophy is a nice way to end a car show, but the real reward is spending time with fellow car owners and admiring their cars.

Since that day I've changed my car show attending pattern. I usually arrive an hour or two after the show has started, and I usually leave early. A few weeks ago I arrived at a small show at 11:00 a.m. and left at 2:00 p.m. At 4:00 p.m. a friend called to tell me that my car had won first place in its class.

I have not yet bothered to go get my trophy.

Vino or Vehicle?

A few ago weeks Mrs. Lambert and I returned from two weeks in Italy where we joined the camera-carrying crowd and did all that is expected of good tourists--walked across Vatican Square, cruised the canals of Venice, admired David and, when necessary, rode in trains, planes and automobiles.

Early in the trip we had been invited by Italian friends to join them in Rome for dinner at their favorite pasta palace. They picked us up at our hotel and off we rode in their new Ford Focus. We traveled all the way to Italy and ended up in a Ford! Not a Ferrari, Fiat or Alpha, but a Ford. Oh well. The owner, Stephano, navigated the cobblestone streets of Rome in his Ford chariot as well as any Ferrari driver. Until the evening's outing we had only seen the traffic through the eyes of a pedestrian. Now we saw it through the windshield as our chauffeur expounded on the merits of Italian motoring styles.

Driving the roads of Italy seems to be more of a controlled chaos ballet rather than just a drive from the villa to the Vatican. The cars and motor scooters are everywhere at the same time and they frequently do things like drive into the oncoming lane in heavy downtown traffic to pass other vehicles. At first glance it seems dangerous, but it quickly becomes apparent that the drivers are experts at maneuvering around other vehicles and pedestrians. The traffic flow reminded me of water flowing down a streambed. The current travels gracefully around any obstacles and every drop of water continues on its way. Even the pedestrians crossing the streets will confidently jump into the traffic stream and quickly make their way across the thoroughfare with little impediment to the vehicles or damage to themselves.

Two other things became apparent as we observed the traffic in Rome and Florence: the majority of cars are very small, and when not in use, most are parked everywhere imaginable on the streets. The few garages we noticed on our endless walks were frequently filled with grapes hanging from the ceilings and piled in baskets. The resulting glut of individual cars parked along the curbs have to be small in order to fit into the few spaces available. The small streets, restrictive automobile taxes and high gas prices also make small cars a wise choice.

Sometimes the streets looked like the aftermath of a flood. Cars were parked along the road at different angles, some backed straight in like motorcycles, some parallel, some in the opposite direction to the traffic flow and some perpendicular to other cars. It looked a bit random, but it resulted in every available space being utilized for car storage.

Leaving the large cities and traveling to the rural areas  revealed more garages. They, like the cars, were usually very small and, like in the larger towns, were occasionally decorated with hanging vino ingredients that left no room for parking a car. Many of the homes with garages appeared to be of newer construction compared to other nearby garageless residences. That means some homes are only 100 years old rather than 300 years old.

Our final destination was Venice, where there are no cars, so no garages are necessary. Perhaps the gondoliers need someplace to park their gondolas.

It seems that not owning a car and not needing a place to store a vehicle means that there is more room for vino storage. Some people may feel that this is a fair trade.

Swap Meet Bargains?

The Buick sign that I bought at the swap meet for only $40 actually cost me $88. How did that happen? Let me explain.

Many members of the collector car community consider attending automotive swap meets to be as much fun as a day at the circus. There are sights, sounds and smells that can only be found in a huge field and large buildings filled with  rusty old cars and parts, beat up old signs and the aroma of bad swap meet food. Car nuts will drive for many miles in search of an elusive part or a bargain-priced collector car.

Last month my friend Greg and I attended the Portland Swap Meet. This annual (48th year) meet is held in Oregon at the Portland Expo Center and the nearby Portland International Raceway track. It is the largest automotive swap meet in the Northwest and one of the largest on the West Coast. This is the 14th year that I've attended, and it usually takes three long days just to cover the entire area. I've returned home with everything from just the souvenir swap-meet button to a 1950 Studebaker and a 1960 Thunderbird.

Any swap-meet veteran will tell you that finding something to spend your money on is only part of the reason to attend. While there you'll see car buddies, look at great cars, and attend the usual post-swap-meet social gatherings. Swap meets are always mini-vacations for the vintage vehicle crowd. Small swap meets provide a morning's activities and large swap meets are like spending a few days in a Disneyland filled with collector cars and hard-to-find parts.

My recent swap-meet sojourn resulted in the acquisition of a large Buick dealership sign, an old hand-painted double-sided no-parking sign, an original poster for the 1965 Pacific Raceways "Seattle Seafair Trophy Race" and an award presented in 1963 to the Delaney Ford dealership for "Distinguished Achievement." It is very likely that I could live without these items being displayed in my already

overflowing garage, and my long suffering bride always has the same question about my latest additions: "Where are you going to put them?" I always remind her that the garage is actually a large Rubik's Cube and I just need to keep shifting things around until everything is in its proper place.

So how did I do as far as getting some bargains? At $40 the Buick sign was a great deal. The no-parking sign was fairly priced at $40, the trophy race sign at $25 was likely just under "market value" and the Ford dealership award at $15 was another bargain. The Lambert garage has some fun new additions and my wallet is only $120 lighter. Or was that the actual cost?

My share of the gas was about $50 and meals during the swap-meet adventure cost about $120. Some good friends invited us to stay at their home, and in return a few of their meals were paid for out of my wallet to the tune of about $60. The total of $230 added to the cost of the swap-meet "bargains" results in an average cost of about $88 per item. This is a bit high for at least three of the items but, as mentioned earlier, going to a swap meet is not just about finding bargains or elusive parts. Along with acquiring the signs came lots of laughs with good friends, a few days away from the office, expansion of my knowledge about old cars and parts, and some cool display items for the garage.

Yes, my purchases were truly bargains. Now where the heck can I find a space for them?

Grubby to Guggenheim

The empty beer bottles have been put in the recycling, the stained pizza boxes thrown into the compost bin and the Avanti hubcap used as a potato chip bowl is again hanging on the wall. The bachelor party for my friend Brian is now history and my garage can relax until the next excuse to fill it with friends. As a confirmed garageophile I enjoy having visitors, and I let friends know that drop-ins are always welcome.

But not all garageophiles are like me. In fact, garageophiles come in several types.

One type is the "Hermit" who displays a collection of automotive and petroleum memorabilia in the garage and then posts a "No Trespassing" sign on the door. This type reminds me of Gollum from the "Lord of the Rings" who cries out "She's mine, my pretty, all mine!" as he holds the ring close to his chest. The Gollums take great pleasure in enjoying their collection solo, and they, of course, have every right to be lone wolves.

Another type is the "Museum Curator" who keeps the garage looking like an operating room at Johns Hopkins Hospital. The lighting is perfect, the counters and floors are spotless and everything is placed in a well thought-out location. The garage's "feng shui," or energy flow, is perfect and the feeling upon entering is similar to entering the Guggenheim Museum and admiring a Mondrian, except the work of art displayed in the garage is more likely a "Best in Class" award from Pebble Beach or an original Ed Roth T-shirt. The curator's door is usually open to friends, but be sure to wipe your feet before you step inside the garage.

Perhaps a more common garage atmosphere is that of the "Oiled Hand Henrys" in the hobby. Upon entering, you notice the smell of gasoline, oil and dirty rags. The counters are stacked and strewn with various projects, the walls display old signs that were procured for free when they were new signs, and visitors are told, "Go ahead and move that stuff off the chair and have a seat. Beer?" The Henrys love to have friends drop in and their garages are frequently the evening and weekend destination for car buddies.

The "Man Cave" and "Garagemahal" trend has resulted in many garageophiles putting considerable thought into the use and appearance of what, to others, is just a storage area for lawn mowers, bicycles, Christmas decorations and things that are too good to throw away but not good enough to keep.

How should the garage be decorated and utilized? Do you prefer a hermit cave, operating room or museum? Do you want the garage to be your private rabbit hole or a place where friends and visitors are always welcome? Will the floors and counters become messy as a result of your current restoration project or will it be a spotless area that includes a dust filter and wall-to-wall chrome and glass display cases?

They are all good! Hermit or Henry, grubby or Guggenheim, the personal pleasure gained from a personalized garage is just that, personal. Surround it with barbed wire or open the doors to guests, it's your choice. Just get out there and enjoy your garage!

Going Back

There's an old cliché that states "You can't go home again." You can.

Forty-nine years ago five friends from Tacoma and I started a group called the Steeds Car Club. I've written about it in past columns so I'll be brief with the details. The club quickly grew to about 15 members, was very active in the Seattle/Tacoma hot-rod scene and stayed active until the late 1970s. The membership over those years changed but a consistent number of approximately 15 members at any time seemed to be the norm. Most of the members were only active in the club during their high school years, after which they went off to college, the military or whatever direction young adulthood took them. For most of us, those years of wearing club jackets while participating in car activities formed wonderful memories and, most importantly, helped to seal lifelong bonds with the other members.

Fast forward to early 2010 when a couple of the original Steeds members decided to see if there was any interest in getting the past members together to re-form the club. Many of the members were retired or nearing retirement and had more spare time to enjoy life. The two members spread the word that a gathering of past members was being organized and anyone interested was invited to attend. The expectation was that four or five members would likely show up. The day arrived and past members began pulling into the parking lot at an automotive facility in Puyallup, WA. The expected four or five former Steeds quickly grew to 16 members and friends. The enthusiasm for bringing life back into the club was overwhelming and 16 hands went into the air voting to re-form the club.

There are now 70 members and each month there are one or two club activities with 10 to 40 of the members participating. We reproduced our old car club jackets, and a few members still have their original jackets. Amazingly, some of the old jackets still fit!

Why did the club fall back into place so easily and quickly? Most of the group are officially senior citizens and such high school behavior may seem a bit immature to some observers. Imagine a large group of grandparent-aged men and women hanging out together, driving 40- to 75-year-old cars and all wearing matching jackets. It does sound a little silly.

What caused this to happen?

The bonds we formed during our school years are as strong as steel. Several members of the Steeds shared classrooms as far back as grade school. We grew up together and some even went off to college or the military together. A few participated in each other's weddings and babysat each other's children. As time passed a few members remained in close contact, but most drifted apart.

The rapid and successful re-formation of the club is a strong indication of our mutual appreciation of old friends and our desire to reconnect with these friends and create new memories. We learned that the friendships formed in our youth are our strongest friendships.

A wonderful thing happened that is, perhaps, not unusual. Members who had not seen each other in decades immediately regained the close bond with the others in the group. As we were walking around a car show together, Doug and Greg, best friends in junior and senior high school, were laughing and frequently putting their hands on each other's shoulders or playfully punching each other. Bob, my closest friend in high school, would occasionally glance at me with a twinkle in his eye and a knowing smile on his face. We laughed about some of our adventures and marveled at how the decades melted away as the club re-established itself.

Last weekend I found myself at a car show with 13 members of the Steeds. We looked at cars together, got to know each other's spouses a bit better, dined together and, best of all, reclaimed the closeness that we all shared nearly 50 years ago.

Friends and family are two of the best things in life, and

sometimes old friends also become family.

I think the cliché is wrong. You can go "home" again.

PART THREE

TV TIME

In the summer of 1993 my good friend Tim Stansbury and I taped the first episode of what became the *VINTAGE VEHICLE SHOW*. The location was the A&W drive-in located just north of Seattle in the suburb of Shoreline. Tim was running a local television station so we broadcast the show and, much to our pleasure, received a lot of support and encouragement to tape another show. We took that advice and as of this writing we have been on the air  for 20 years and recently produced our 440th episode of the show. The next few stories are related to the various things that have happened to us while producing the show.

Whoops! I Dropped a Name

Some of you are familiar with the *Vintage Vehicle Show*, a television show that I have hosted and co-produced with Tim Stansbury for the past 20 years. This internationally broadcast show features coverage of car shows, automobile museums, collections and automotive restoration shops. The consistent thread in the show is the 1500 interviews I have done over the years. The two questions most often asked by viewers are, "What was he/she really like?" and "Who was your favorite guest on the show?"

What follows is a partial answer to these questions and a heavy dose of name dropping.

JAY LENO - *Tonight Show* host, comedian and total car nut: Jay was appearing at a car show in Pasadena and was gracious enough to agree to an interview. We talked about the car hobby, his massive car collection, the breakdown of his 1928 Bugatti on the way to the interview and his views about people at car shows. Jay's most memorable comment was, "At some shows the cars on display are unprotected because the audience respects the cars and knows that they should not touch them. At other shows there's someone leaning on your pristine 1956 Chevrolet and when you ask the person not to lean on the car he gets all huffy and stomps off."

Jay was funny, cooperative and, most impressively, very gracious to everyone at the show seeking his attention. One person walked up and began telling him a long story about mistaking someone at a bar for Jay. The longer the story went on, the more obvious it became that the storyteller was not of sound mind. Jay respectfully thanked him for his story and politely extracted himself from the situation.

One of the best things about having Jay on the show is the credibility that it gives. For years I was asked, "Has Jay Leno been on your show?" The implication was that the show was not a real show until Jay was a guest. Now, when I answer yes to the question, people respond in a way that implies that they feel the show is a legitimate show about old cars.

CHIP FOOSE - *Overhaulin'* television show host and world-renowned custom car designer: Chip has been my guest on the show three times, and the most obvious observation I can make about him is his enthusiasm for the hobby. He loves cars and car people and will

spend hours talking to his peers and admirers about anything car related. The cliché of "A car guy's car guy" is totally appropriate.

The first *Vintage Vehicle Show* interview I conducted with Chip was at the 2002 Grand National Roadster Show

in San Mateo, CA. He did a great job of keeping his cool as I addressed him as "Skip" during the interview.

BOYD CODDINGTON - *American Hot Rod* television show host and custom car builder: Boyd was famous for building great cars and for rarely ever laughing. He agreed to allow us to tape an interview with him in his shop in La Habra, CA and to tape the monthly car show that he held in his parking lot. He was very serious during our visit but was also very open and willing to give us as much of his time as we needed to tape the show. I did get him to laugh a couple of times during the interview, so he's not stone faced all of the time.

After the interview I went into his gift shop to buy a large Boyd Coddington Wheels sign. Boyd walked in and told the clerk not to charge me for it and to ship it for free. I asked him to autograph it "To the Vintage Vehicle Show" which he did, although he misspelled vehicle. Boyd passed away in 2008.

GEORGE BARRIS - Perhaps the most famous of all custom car builders: His most famous car, the Batmobile, was transformed by George in 1966 from what had been the Ford Company's 1955 Futura show car. Several years ago George did two quick interviews for me when he was appearing at the Seattle Roadster Show. One afternoon I was lucky enough to sit with him during a press luncheon and thoroughly enjoyed his great stories about the early days of custom car building.

A few years ago I tried very hard to get an interview with George at his shop in Hollywood. He would not return my calls or email messages. A few weeks later the crew and I were filming at a museum nearby and, when we finished, we decided to just stop by

George's shop and try to talk him into doing an interview. I walked in, introduced myself and mentioned that he'd done two interviews previously and that we'd had lunch together a few years earlier. He didn't remember me or my TV show and he was not interested in doing an interview. He seemed angry and began reading a car magazine, likely hoping that I'd take the hint and leave him alone. It was looking hopeless until his assistant looked at me and said, "Oh, you're that really nice guy on TV. George, get off of your ass and give him an interview!" George put on his iconic George Barris sunglass/hat/gold jacket combination, looked into the camera and gave me a great interview.

I saw George recently at a car show in Portland, OR. He walked up, shook my hand and told me how much he enjoys the TV show.

GENE WINFIELD - Considered to be one of the best custom car designers and builders in the world: A few of the better known people in the car hobby are good designers but don't know which end of a hammer or paint sprayer to hold. Gene knows everything about everything when it comes to car building and he builds the cars himself. He is 84 years old and looks more like 64. His cars are best noted for always looking in style and freshly built, despite when they may have been designed and constructed. The cars, like Gene, don't seem to age. He's been a guest on the show four times and each interview was enlightening and entertaining.

Gene shared a story with my about appearing at a car show

and being approached by a young couple. The guy asked Gene to autograph his girlfriend's shoulder. Gene happily scrawled his signature on her shoulder and the couple seemed very excited about

GENE WINFIELD
Custom Builder

it. The next day they came back to the weekend event to show Gene her new tattoo. The previous evening they had gone to a tattoo shop and had Gene's signature tattooed on her shoulder.

JOHN D'AGOSTINO – Several "big time" car culture icons have made more than one appearance on the show. John D'Agostino holds the record with 9 appearances on the show. John seems to be everywhere at the same time. One weekend he's appearing at the Grand National Roadster Show and a week later he's displaying his cars at a show in Norway. A week later he's schmoozing at an East Coast show and then he's off to Germany to display his talents. I have interviewed him many times because he's a great guy that knows how to make even greater cars out of great cars. His specialty is turning luxury cars into mild to wild

customs. Anything John touches is transformed into an iconic custom within the hobby.

Other guests with names worth dropping who have appeared

on the show include Vic Edelbrock, Troy Ladd, Jimmy White, Mike Lavallee, Troy Trepanier, Steve Frisbie, Bruce Meyer, Dennis Gage, Elvira, Barry Maguire, Steve Saleen, Voodoo Larry, Ed Justice, Joe Bailon, Norm Grabowski, Bones Noteboom, Heidi VanHorn, Randy Clark, Jim Wangers, Cindy Williams, Paul LeMat, Candy Clark and many other car-culture celebrities. Famous or non-famous, all the guests have been greatly appreciated and have graciously shared their views about every aspect of the car hobby.

You are perhaps wondering who was my favorite all-time guest? I'd have to say Marysville, WA resident Barry Hilbert.

BARRY HILBERT – Barry is not a celebrity, famous collector or custom car builder. He's just a simple and gracious man who knows a lot about cars. His collection includes a 1959 Lincoln convertible, 1959 Thunderbird convertible and two King Midget convertibles. He had the answer to any automotive question asked but eagerly sought out any additional information that he might discover from our conversation. Barry's choice of cars is an excellent illustration of how broad is his appreciation of the automobile.

We have produced over 440 episodes of the *Vintage Vehicle Show* and I consider all of the guests to be "celebrities."

Landing Leno

There are two famous car collectors in the old car hobby--Jay Leno and all the rest. Jay's collection includes everything from the rarest and most desirable classic cars to ponderous American behemoths from the 1950s and 1960s. Anyone unaware of Jay's love of cars is likely living on a small Pacific Rim island waiting for WWII to end.

I started courting Jay about four years ago when it became apparent that he was willing to appear on every TV car show in existence except mine. An inside source supplied me with his personal secretary's phone number and the onslaught began. Helga, also known as "The Gatekeeper," began receiving calls from my personal secretary, also known as me, requesting an interview with Mr. Leno. I was told that he was much too busy and to try again some other time. The other time arrived a few weeks later when I told Helga that I would be in California soon and would be able to schedule an interview with her boss. She asked me to email the request so she could pass it on to Jay. I admired her creative way of saying "No, and please stop bugging me." I sent the request into email outer darkness and, no surprise, received no response.

Helga received phone calls from me every few months and, much to her credit, was always polite when she informed me that Mr. Leno was still much too busy for the likes of me. Then a small miracle happened; I received an invitation from Helga to attend a broadcast of the *Tonight Show* and meet with Jay after the show. I was so excited that I had to breathe into a paper bag for a while after the call.

A few days later I was off to the NBC studio in Burbank to watch the show and throw down a few brewskies with my new best buddy Jay; however, it didn't quite turn out that way. I was able to chat with him after the show and talk about favorite cars and mutual friends. When I asked him for an interview he said, "We can do that. Just arrange it with Helga." Pooh!

My calls to her were received with the same previous lack of cooperation. I vowed to wait until the *Vintage Vehicle Show* was so successful that Jay would have to call my personal secretary and beg for me to be a guest on his show. That has yet to happen.

Fast forward to last Sunday, when the *Vintage Vehicle Show* crew was in Pasadena filming the Art Center Classic Car Show. Many big-name car guys were there and I was able to tape interviews with Chip Foose, Barry MeGuiar, Bruce Meyer and a few other automotive notables. Then it happened; Jay arrived. He drove up in a 1928 Bugatti, and believe me, he was noticed. All eyes were on Jay and people moved quickly to be closer to him. I was much more subtle; I ran over women and children to try to get an interview.

He stated, or lied, that he enjoyed our last conversation and agreed to do the interview. I feared that I'd again be hyperventilating due to being so excited to have him on the *Vintage Vehicle Show.*

The crew set up the equipment and I proceeded to successfully glean from Jay such pearls as "I like the Art Center show because you don't have to worry about someone leaning against your car, smoking a cigarette and wondering why you think it's wrong for them to be rubbing their butt on your $40,000 paint job." We talked about the car hobby and he shared a few humorous stories about some of his automotive adventures. We finished the interview, I thanked him, and we both went on with our day.

Now I reply to a question frequently asked, "Yes, as a matter of fact Jay Leno has been a guest on my show."

Epilogue: Jay recently made his second appearance on the *Vintage Vehicle Show* when he was interviewed by our "cub reporter" Ryan Haarsager.

Fire! Fire!

I'd never seen fiberglass burn before, but I got to do that one day when I was hosting television's *Vintage Vehicle Show*. The fiberglass looked like layers of a newspaper curling up as it was destroyed by the flames.

Let me explain what happened. Hosting the show for nearly two decades has allowed me to visit hundreds of automotive museums, private collections, restoration facilities and garages containing the simplest to the most sophisticated vehicles in the world. We've featured everything from restoration projects in single car garages to vast collections housed in enormous airplane hangars and multi-story structures. Almost every building was well organized, clean and equipped with necessary safety items such as sprinkler systems and fire extinguishers. But another necessary fire safety item is the awareness that these safety features are available. Unfortunately, on one particular day I was unaware.

Some of the information that I'm about to share with you will be a bit vague because I don't want any of the participants to lose their jobs. I also do not want to be involved in any automobile owner's future "diminished value" lawsuit.

We frequently end *Vintage Vehicle Show* episodes by thanking my guest, saying goodbye to the audience and driving off in an interesting vehicle that was featured during the episode. On this particular day I chose a very rare sports car manufactured in the 1960s. Fewer than 400 of this model were made and they usually sell in the 350K to 750K range. A recent exception to this was a sale of over one million dollars for a pristine example. The chosen car for the closing shot was an excellent example of this rare vehicle and was also previously owned by a very well known celebrity.

On this day the interviews were with the museum's director and the designer of the rare sports car. After the designer's interview, the vehicle was taken out of the building and readied for driving at the close of the episode. It had not been started for a long time so some extra equipment was needed: battery charger, starter fluid and a little persuading. I remained in the building finishing up the interview with the museum director while the designer and an assistant attempted to awaken the fiberglass beauty from its long nap. It woke up very grouchy.

Suddenly the designer came running into the building calling out the director's name. His tone of voice made it clear that something serious was happening. He should have been yelling "Fire! Fire!" rather than anyone's name.

The interview stopped abruptly and we all ran outside. There, sitting in the parking lot, was my chosen chariot with flames coming from the left front fender and out of the engine compartment. It was not just a small flame, it was large enough for a half dozen people to sit around and roast marshmallows. At first the severity of the situation escaped me because I was fascinated with watching the fiberglass burn. The fender and engine compartment were made of layers of fiberglass, and the layers were melting and curling up as they burned. Then I snapped out of my fascinated stupor and thought, "Now what do I do?"

I ran back into the building to find a fire extinguisher but could not find a single one despite looking everywhere. I ran around the building searching for something that might stop a fire: water, blankets or anything that might extinguish the flames. I ran back out of the building with a large blanket, but by then someone had located a fire extinguisher and put out the flames. The front of the car was a smoldering mess covered in white fire retardant glop.

The designer explained that the carburetion system included an air filter configuration that started in the fender and led to the carburetors. Apparently, gas had built up in the air cleaner and when the battery cables were connected the spark caused an explosion and the fire.

So what's the point of my story other than sharing the danger and excitement experienced in the parking lot? It is that panic can cause a person to suffer from confusion and a form of temporary blindness.

As we returned to the building to finish the interview, I was stunned by what I saw. Every one of the numerous structural support columns in the building had a fire extinguisher mounted on it. Not only that, every post had a large red band painted around it indicating that there was a fire extinguisher on the column. How could I not have seen these?

A good friend and long-time professional fire fighter told me that this is not uncommon. People panic and are overwhelmed with confusion, and a temporary form of restricted vision sets in.

The building containing the car collection was equipped with the necessary fire extinguishers properly displayed and easily accessible. What else could have been done to bring a quicker response to this flaming fiberglass inferno? Maybe if I'd been a bit calmer while under duress I would have helped put out the flames sooner.

This incident had a profound influence on me. I now glance around auto storage facilities to see where the fire extinguishers are located. My garage has four fire extinguishers prominently located and easily accessed.

How many fire extinguishers are in your garage?

A Fan or Afraid

I've driven some exciting cars in my life, but this was the first time that I considered seeking medical attention to recover from the experience.

It was at the Marconi Automotive Museum, located in Tustin, CA, which is a wonderful collection of everything from a 1930s fire engine to exotic cars worth several million dollars. Dick Marconi had invited the *Vintage Vehicle Show* crew to film an episode at his facility, and we jumped at the chance to tour one of America's best automobile collections. You will never meet a more gracious man than Dick and you will rarely have the opportunity to see a collection as varied as the cars displayed at his museum. Included in the collection are go-carts, dragsters, Formula 1 cars, hot rods, customs, muscle cars, classics and sports cars. The collection is surrounded by an equally impressive collection of automotive memorabilia. Dick has brought it all under one very large roof for you to enjoy.

And then there are Dick's Ferraris.

Everyone knows that Ferraris are special. They are expensive to purchase, impractical to own, difficult to maintain and a challenge to keep running properly. They are also one of the world's best combinations of form and function. I will need a substantially better job to afford to park one in my garage, but that doesn't stop me from dreaming of ownership. On this sunny summer day I was given the opportunity to get behind the wheel of Italy's finest and be an "owner" for a brief time.

Dick finished being our tour guide and we then prepared for the final scene in the episode. We frequently end the show with me climbing into a car, saying goodbye to the viewers and driving towards the horizon. Dick handed me the keys to his 1997 Ferrari 550 Maranello. It is amazing what Enzo Ferrari could do with some metal, rubber, cowhide and paint. This painfully red Italian stallion was off the chart for beauty and, as was soon demonstrated, performed as well as it looked.

As the cameras were rolling I thanked the viewers, climbed into the car with Dick and drove off. That's when the consideration for medical attention began. This was a car worth more than the combined value of the Lambert Auto Collection (a 1958 rambler and a 7-year-old Taurus station wagon) and the Stately Lambert Manor (the best split-level home the 1970s had to offer). If I wrecked this car my wife would need to get a third job to pay for the damage.

The plan was for the drive to be short, but Dick had other ideas. "Go to the light, turn right and get on it," he said. I turned right and accelerated at a very modest pace. "You are driving like my grandmother; get on it!" Dick was in his 70s at the time and, therefore, his grandmother must have been very old and a very cautious driver. I took the next turn and pushed the gas pedal a bit closer to the carpet. Dick responded with "Look, this is a Ferrari. Ferraris are to be driven like Ferraris, not like Volkswagens. At the next corner I want you to take a right turn and then floor it!" Not only was he providing me the opportunity to see what Enzo had designed, he was demanding it. I did as I was told and quickly learned why diapers are made in adult sizes.

Bracing myself, I shoved the gas pedal to the floor. OH-MY-GAWD! The Ferrari leapt forward so fast that my eyeballs were pushed back in my head. I'm not kidding, that was the sensation. My stomach did a roller coaster flip as the world immediately began

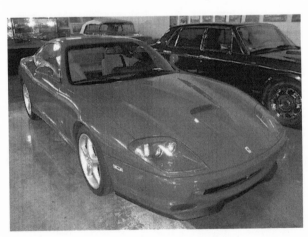

speeding by faster and faster. It impressed me that there was no wheel spinning, "fishtailing" or loss of control. This 12-cylinder-powered rocket ship felt like a giant slot car going nowhere but straight ahead.

I quickly realized that the best plan was to put a stop to this four-wheeled fighter jet before we were either being chased by the local constable or imbedded in the side of a building.

Now I understand the major reason why Ferrari owners pay the price of ownership. Not only is every Ferrari ever manufactured beautiful, they are also faster than a bar of wet soap sliding down the side of an iceberg. I let my eyeballs drop back properly in their sockets and drove cautiously back to the museum. I climbed out of the car much like, I imagined, a fighter pilot after his first training flight.

My stomach settled down, no diapers or medical attention were needed and Dick realized that he had succeeded in recruiting another member into the Ferrari Fan Club.

I wonder if my wife would be willing to put the house up for sale to raise enough for the down payment on a Ferrari?

Your Last Ride

My wife thinks I'm unique. My friends think I'm a bit odd and they are likely correct. So if I think other people are odd then they must be very odd.

Recently the *Vintage Vehicle Show* crew and I were in California to tape a hearse gathering hosted by the Phantom Coaches Hearse Club. Yes, hearses--that big black station wagon that some of us will take a ride in on our last day above ground. Where would you expect a hearse show to happen? Where else but at a graveyard. The Fairhaven Cemetery in Santa Anna was host to the event and it was the perfect location. Before us was a beautiful southern California day and an assortment of 1959 to 1972 Cadillacs lined up next to a huge mausoleum. About a half dozen of these Grim Reaper rods were in very good condition; others ranged from a little rough to something that should have gone into the ground with its last passenger.

I have a strong respect for hearses due to their honorable place in our society and to the quality of their construction. I expected the owners to perhaps be a bit peculiar and I wasn't let down. A few owners sported the attire of 1880s funeral directors. There were lots of shirts and signs with sayings like, "Pass me on the curve; I need the business" and, "Are you dying for a ride in my car." Yes, many of the owners were a bit odd, but they were extremely cordial and as excited about their cars as any other collector car owner.

Several of the hearses were complete with coffins and corpses. Not real corpses, of course, just excellent reproductions. One driver had a corpse sitting up next to him in the passenger seat and another had one looking out the back window and waving. Andy, the name of one deceased rider, was sitting up in his coffin watching television. A thoughtful couple, I think their last name may have been Munster, had two child car seats attached to the floor in the back so their twin daughters could safely ride along. The paint jobs ranged from original black to being covered with hot rod flames. I think it's a bad omen to take your last ride in a flamed hearse. One hearse was painted in green scales and had dozens of lizards painted on the exterior. The owners told me many stories of people's reactions to seeing the cars that varied from receiving single digit salutes to top awards at car shows. The group mentioned that elderly Hispanic women frequently perform the sign of the cross and look down at the ground when passed by one of these graveyard delivery wagons.

My impression of these people was positive. They showed a lot of imagination, excellent senses of humor and a healthy acceptance of the short time each one of us will occupy in the history of humankind.

Would I ever own a hearse? My wife is not that tolerant. Would I voluntarily ride in one? I have several times and will again. Did I think these people were odd? Of course, but it's not often that I get to hang out with people as odd as I am.

Second to None

There is a growing segment of automobile racing known as dwarf car racing. Dwarf cars are replicas of American automobiles manufactured from 1928 through 1948. The designation of dwarf car is due to the requirement that the cars be 48 inches or less in height, 38 inches or less in width and have a 73-inch wheelbase. They can only be powered by four-cycle motorcycle engines of no more than 1220 cubic centimeters. Other rigidly monitored construction requirements assure that they are lightweight, fast and look like go-carts with bodies pounded out of scrap metal. It also assures that they are really fun to drive.

Evergreen Speedway, located in Monroe, WA, occasionally features dwarf car racing events. On one of these occasions I had the pleasure of driving in an exhibition race. The TV show that I host and co-produce, *Vintage Vehicle Show*, was filming an episode about these cars and the track promoters thought it would be a great promotion to have me drive during the evening's halftime intermission. I'm always willing to suspend concerns for my personal safety when it comes to having fun and/or producing an exciting episode of the show.

Dwarf car driver and owner Kurt Wilson was kind enough to allow me to drive his car. The 1200-cc Suzuki-powered 1932 Ford Coupe imitation was rated in second place nationally, so I was fortunate to be in one of the best cars available. Kurt gave me explicit instructions to follow, and not attempt to pass, the only other car on the track, another dwarf car driven by a racing veteran. It was lucky for the other guy, because it's a sure thing that I, with my total lack of experience, would have trounced him thoroughly and ended up in the winner's circle covered with kisses from the trophy girl.

Kurt had radio contact with the other driver, and a signaling system was set up among the three of us. Kurt would be standing by the track at the straightaway, and I was to give him one of three hand signals when I drove past him--right-hand thumb up if I wanted to go faster, thumb down if slower and my hand going from side to side if I wanted to get the heck off the track. These hand gestures were radioed to the driver in front who would, depending on these gestures, speed up, slow down or meet me back in the pits and make chicken clucking noises at me as I returned from the track.

OK, drop that flag and let me show the world what an amazing driver looks like.

My first impression was that this car was very fast. It accelerated rapidly and I drove as fast as I could. These cars are engineered exceptionally well, and this was manifested, in part, by the feeling that the car was riding on railroad tracks. There was no slipping and sliding; it dug in and took off.

My competitor was squarely in my sights as if he were on the wrong end of a WWII dogfight. You're mine, Mr. Fancy-pants race car driver, and I'm about to shoot you down. We'd completed one lap and I decided to signal to Kurt what I was really made of. He saw my thumb-up signal and radioed my impending dogfight victim of my desire to go faster. That was the last time I saw the other car or driver. He shot off like I was standing at a bus stop and he was flying by in a Messerschmitt. I pushed the little dwarf car as fast as I dared, but to no avail, the other guy just disappeared somewhere over the horizon.

I was sure that I was traveling at speeds of well over 100 miles per hour, but Kurt later said my top speed was 85 mph. I made about six laps of the track before Kurt signaled that my brief career as a race car driver had come to an end. The other driver was already back in the pits and had been there long enough to have dinner, shower and catch a little TV in his trailer before I'd completed the same number of laps as he had. There was no trophy girl with puckered lips waiting for me and I swear I could hear the sound of a chicken clucking.

Well, heck, what did anyone expect? The last race that I'd participated in was aboard my Schwinn Black Phantom bicycle while racing Ronnie Petersen who was piloting his sister's Disney Princess bicycle. Do you have any idea how humiliating it is to get beaten by a creepy girl's bike? It's about as humiliating as it is to finish last in a dwarf car race.

Hey, wait; I was driving the second car to finish the race. That means I took second place in my very first auto racing event. Not bad!

Gears and Grins

You have just arrived on the planet Zorgda and Buck Rodgers has handed over the keys to his rocket ship with the instructions, "Be back in a half an hour and don't burn up the afterblasters."

That's how I felt on this particular sunny morning in Irvine, CA.

While co-producing and hosting television's *Vintage Vehicle Show*, I've found myself in many great situations: touring very impressive private car collections, racing at a NASCAR event, visiting with Jay Leno and touring his collection, having lunch with George Barris, flying to car shows in the back of bi-planes and being given the keys to some of the automotive world's most desirable cars.

Since 1984 Steve Saleen has been the designer and manufacturer of the famous Saleen Mustangs. Ford supplies him with the cars and he then supplies the public with a car that defines the term "Muscle Car." I have had the pleasure of owning a 1988 Saleen and will swear on a stack of car magazines that Steve knows how to turn a good car into a great car. Now he has joined with world-famous race car driver Parnelli Jones to create the Saleen/Parnelli Jones Mustang. How smart is Steve? Smart enough to team up with Mr. Jones and create a muscle car combining the styling cues of Parnelli's world-conquering 1970 Boss 302 Mustang with the modern technology of the Ford/Saleen marriage. How dumb is Steve? Dumb enough to have his assistant give me the keys along with the instructions, "Be back in a half an hour and don't burn up the tires." I was out the factory door and in the car before the sentence was finished. Just being able to climb into the car took my breath away. Turning the key started a symphony that was an audio combination of the Rolling Stones playing real rock and roll and hand grenades exploding. I pulled out of the driveway, drove just out of view, and put my right foot to the floor. The car rocketed forward like a Blue Angel on a sunny day while staying stuck to the concrete like bubblegum to a tennis shoe. I felt totally in control as I went through the gears and the grins. The Saleen factory is located in an industrial area of Irvine that provides winding roads and few stop lights. Going through the gears of the five-speed manual transmission, I created enough endorphins and testosterone to float the QE2.

One half hour later I joined Steve Saleen as he gave the *Vintage Vehicle Show* viewers a tour of the Saleen factory. There are eight stations within the facility that transform an already amazing Mustang into a Saleen/Parnelli Jones Mustang. The original suspension and motor are replaced with race-engineered equipment that Steve and Parnelli feel is just the thing to liven up a weekend. The 302 cubic-inch 400-horsepower V8 will remind you of why many old muscle cars now sell for over $1,000,000. This power source, along with the Saleen-designed interior seating and exterior front and rear panels, will be appreciated both on your neighborhood streets and at race courses across the nation.

What was my overall impression of my day with Steve Saleen? Last week I traded in my 1988 Mustang for an almost new Mustang. Not a Saleen/Parnelli Jones Mustang, but one step closer.

Karma Cash

Most people have a fantasy about finding a dusty item at a garage sale that turns out to be worth thousands of dollars. We all want to be that person on *Antiques Roadshow* who is told the vase purchased for $10 is actually worth $10,000. Well, I was lucky enough to be with my friend Gary when he had such an experience.

A few days ago the crew and I returned from taping six *Vintage Vehicle Show* episodes in California and Nevada. One of the episodes was at the home of Gary Wales, noted collector of everything from 700-year-old weapons to anything automotive. His eclectic collection includes J.P. Morgan's first driver's license, and huge double doors that once provided entry to a Spanish castle. His car collection includes a few ancient Bentleys, Rolls Royces, and LaFrance fire trucks that have been converted into whimsical vehicles resembling the star car from the movie *Chitty Chitty Bang Bang*.

On the day we were taping, Gary mentioned that he was waiting for the results of the Bonhams auction in London. Gary's print of the "Bluebird" by Cyril Edward Power, which he had purchased two decades earlier for

$30, was up for auction. The subject of the print, Sir Malcolm Campbell's "Bluebird" race car, had set the world's land speed record in 1935 by reaching 276 miles per hour.

The print had hung on Gary's garage wall for 20 years and had once been offered to a collector in France for $100. The collector's response to Gary's offer was, "Why do you show me this junk? Take it away!" I suspect that this collector has recently worn out a pair of shoes from repeatedly kicking himself in the rear.

We were in Gary's memorabilia-filled garage taping his interview when he received the email informing him that the print had sold for $91,200. He and his chief mechanic looked at the computer screen, looked at each other, looked back at the screen and then began "high fiving" each other. His $30 purchase had turned into one of the best investments that he had ever made.

Gary quickly calmed down and we continued taping the interview.

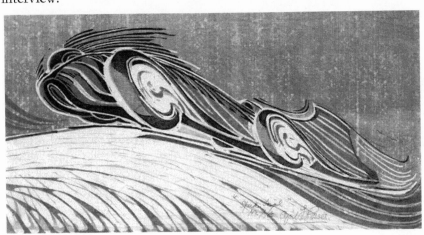

Was this the only time he had such luck? No, it was not. Gary has the ability to successfully do what the rest of us dream of doing.

Many years ago he was enthusiastically admiring an ancient race car owned by legendary race car designer, builder and driver Briggs Cunningham. Briggs noted Gary's interest in this particular car and asked if he wanted to purchase it. Gary responded, "I don't have anywhere near the money needed to buy this car."

Briggs replied, "Go home, gather as much money as you can, put it in a paper bag and bring it back to me."

Gary spent two days trying to raise enough money to buy the

car but was only able to come up with a small fraction of what the car was actually worth. As instructed, he put the cash into a paper bag and went back to Briggs Cunningham's home. "I was not able to raise anywhere near what that car is worth," he said.

Briggs responded, "I'll be the judge of that." He then took the bag, glanced in and proclaimed, "That is exactly what I want for the car!" He didn't even bother to count the money in the bag.

When I asked Gary how he had accumulated his vast collection, he replied, "A lot of this stuff just seems to find me. It seems that I have good karma."

Good things happen to good people, and Gary is the epitome of the cliché "The nicest guy that you will ever meet." He deserves bus loads of good karma.

We finished taping, I thanked Gary for his hospitality and again congratulated him on his windfall. Fantasies of finding $30 items worth $91,200 filled our minds as we drove away.

Before returning to Seattle I stopped in an antique mall and purchased two paintings for $18 each. These original oil paintings each depict a 1930s era Bugatti automobile parked on a country road.

Yes, my fingers are crossed.

Vocal Viewers

This is the 20th year of the *Vintage Vehicle Show* and most of the people that I've had on the show or have met as a result of hosting the show have been very nice. Some, however, have been a bit peculiar.

Once, while waiting for a flight, I was approached by a stranger who greeted me with the comment, "You are not as fat as you look on television." That was his opening line; no hello, no introduction, just the comment about my size. I thanked him and quickly walked away.

We were taping a car show and I approached a car builder and asked to interview him about a car that he had on display. He said no in a very strong manner. I saw him several times over the next few hours and, just for fun, each time asked him again for an interview. I thought I was being very clever and he thought I was being very annoying. He approached me at the end of the car show and quietly said, "You know, I could kick your ass if I wanted to." My guess was that he was correct in his assessment and didn't think that I was very clever. I didn't ask him again for an interview.

Occasionally, people mistake me for a real celebrity and ask for my autograph. I've signed photos, dashboards, sun visors, fenders, hoods, trunk lids and engine compartments. At one show a woman walked up and asked me to autograph her arm. I wondered what part of her anatomy she would have asked me to autograph if I was a big league celebrity.

At another show a woman approached me with something clenched in her hand. This woman had previously sent me a few emails letting me know that she would be attending the show and had a surprise for me. She called out my name and walked up to the stage from where I was emceeing. She hugged me and then took my hand, placed something in it, closed my hand tightly and then walked away. When I opened my hand I was looking at a small triangle of cloth that had at one time been the crotch portion of a pair of panties.

A prison inmate serving his sentence in a Washington State prison wrote and demanded that I send him two pictures of cars every week. "I like muscle cars and especially GTOs, so send mostly GTO pictures." Somehow I lost his address.

Sometimes car owners do not want viewers to know where their collections are located. We taped a large classic car collection and, per the owner's request, gave the location as Ducette, WA. There is no such city but I do have collector car friends with the last name of Ducette. After the show was broadcast, a viewer contacted me to find out where Ducette was located. "I've looked everywhere but I can't find a city by that name," he said. "I think you made it up!" My friends thought it was great that a make-believe city was named after them.

A viewer contacted me to express his opinion that I did not use the English language properly on the show. "You are on television and have the responsibility to use the English language correctly," he told me. I said that I'd do my best and I ain't heard from him since.

Occasionally, media maven Kristyn Burtt guest hosts an episode of the *Vintage Vehicle Show*. She is a tremendously talented interviewer and, in fact, may be too good. Twice we've been contacted about taping car shows and the callers say, "Don't send us that guy. We want Kristyn to do the show." Maybe someday I will be the guest host on her show.

My favorite viewer comment came from a gentleman who took issue with the name of the show. He wrote us a letter complaining, "None of the cars are truly vintage vehicles," and criticized a few other things about the show. Some of his comments were written in all capital letters, some in all capitals and also underlined and some all capitalized, underlined and followed by several exclamation marks. I read the letter on the show while holding an old fashioned brass and rubber bulb horn. I told the viewers that while reading the letter I'd honk the horn once if one of the comments was in capitals, honk it twice if capitals and underlined and three times if capitals, underlined and exclamation marks. It quickly sounded like a 1915 traffic jam in the studio. We could barely get through the letter because the crew and I were laughing so hard. I didn't get a second letter from this critic.

One of the most often heard compliments about the show is for our choice of music. Most episodes have one or two short music montages that feature various shots of cars. Hundreds of people over the years have expressed how much they enjoy the music heard during these montages. The music is usually older style rock and roll, often with a surf music influence. The odd part is that many people have also complained about our choice of music. We have no plans on changing the choice of music anytime soon.

We greatly appreciate hearing from and meeting the viewers of the show. Comments--whether compliments or complaints--let us know that someone is actually watching. For this we are very grateful.

Acknowledgements

This book would not have been written without the help of numerous people. My thanks go to the various magazines, newspapers and web sites that decided my writing was worthy of publication. Authors David Dickinson, Alyce Cornyn-Selby, Julia Radar Detering and Kathleen Fullerton Bernhard provided me with encouragement and inspiration. Nancy Wick of Enlightened Edits made sure that it was not apparent that I did very poorly in English classes during my high school and college years. Author, television reporter and very good friend M.J. McDermott encouraged, pushed, prodded and badgered me into beginning and completing this book. The good people at Wooded Isle Press gave me the opportunity to fulfill my dream of having a book published.

Tim Stansbury, producer of television's *Vintage Vehicle Show*, has been at my side for 25 years. He is a friend, professional inspiration and a person that I respect and admire. We have spent dozens of hours together in traffic jams.

A huge thank you goes to both of my families. My wife and daughter helped me complete the book by blending a perfect mixture of support, encouragement and love. My other family, the Steeds Car Club, has for decades given me friendship, love and laughter. Many of the adventures in this book were enjoyed with one or more members by my side.

The most important word in the title of this book is *FRIENDS*. My biggest thank you of all goes to all of the friends in this book. Thank you for the memories and smiles. Let's make a few more.

ABOUT THE AUTHOR

Lance Lambert's automotive writing began reaching the public in 1995 when *Old Cars Weekly* published his story about the Steeds Car Club. Old Cars Weekly continued publishing his writings as have other publications including *Garage Style, Mustang Times, Mustang News, Journal Newspapers, CruZin', Hot Rod Hotline* and numerous other print and on-line publications. He has been an automotive columnist for the Journal Newspapers since 2004 and for Garage Style magazine since 2008.

Lance was inducted into the Washington Hot Rod Hall of Fame in 2008 and received The Lee Iacocca Award in 2010. This award, presented by the Iacocca Family Foundation, was given to Lance for *"...Dedication to Excellence in Perpetuating an American Automotive Tradition."*

Lance's "day job" is being the executive producer and on-camera host of television's *Vintage Vehicle Show.* Over 440 episodes have been produced since the show began in 1993. The show is broadcast weekly on over 100 stations nationwide and is also seen in 27 foreign markets.

Lance is currently working on his next book, *TRAIN FROM TACOMA: Confessions of a Temporary Hobo.*

Additional information about Lance can be found at www.lance-lambert.com and www.vintagevehicletv.com. Contact John McLean Media at www.johnmcleanmedia.com for information about broadcasting the *Vintage Vehicle Show.*

Also Available

Vintage Vehicle Productions has produced three boxed sets of DVDs. These award winning productions feature Lance Lambert taking you to the best car shows, automotive museums and private automotive collections in the nation. *AMERICA'S CLASSIC CARS, AMERICA'S AUTOMOTIVE MUSEUMS AND CLASSIC CHROME* are distributed by Topics Entertainment and available through Amazon.com and at hundreds of retail and on-line outlets.

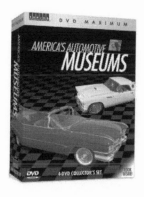
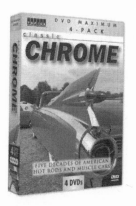

Made in the USA
San Bernardino, CA
21 November 2013